CAMBRIDGE
MIDDLE
ENGLISH
LYRICS

CAMBRIDGE MIDDLE ENGLISH LYRICS

Revised Edition

Edited by

HENRY A. PERSON

GREENWOOD PRESS, PUBLISHERS
NEW YORK

Revised Edition Copyright © 1962
by the University of Washington Press

Reprinted by permission
of the University of Washington Press

First Greenwood Reprinting 1969

Library of Congress Catalogue Card Number 74-88919

SBN 8371-2242-2

PRINTED IN UNITED STATES OF AMERICA

INTRODUCTION

The present collection consists of sixty-seven Middle English poems from MSS. in the Cambridge University library and in the libraries of several colleges of the University. Some years ago Professor Frank A. Patterson of Columbia University and the late Dean Frederick M. Padelford of the University of Washington secured photostatic copies of the MSS. and started the preliminary work of transcription and identification. Presently, however, Mr. Patterson became so occupied with the Columbia Edition of the Works of John Milton, and Dr. Padelford with the *Variorum Spenser*, that they were unable to give the necessary time and effort to the Cambridge poems. A few years before his death, Dr. Padelford, who always had a soft spot in his heart for Middle English lyric poetry, made the photostats available to the present editor, at that time a student in his Spenser seminar. Although I worked at the task as diligently as possible, the war and the pressure of other duties delayed publication until the present time. Sixty of the poems are here printed for the first time; the remaining seven have been included for reasons indicated in the Notes.

Carleton F. Brown's *Religious Lyrics of the Fifteenth Century*, Richard L. Greene's *The Early English Carols*, Henry N. MacCracken's second volume of Lydgate's minor poems, and Rossell H. Robbins' *Secular Lyrics of the XIV and XV Centuries*, all of which appeared during the course of my labors, have greatly simplified my task by the light they have shed on the period and the genre, and have reduced somewhat the number of poems to be handled. A further reduction was achieved by abandoning one part of the plan of my predecessors, who had intended to present not only hitherto unprinted poems, but also such poems as had been printed from other MSS. but not collated with the Cambridge copies. Such a collation is as desirable now as ever, but in view of the steadily

rising cost of bookmaking, it will probably be wiser to publish the collations by themselves in an article or two than to print the entire poems.

As the Notes indicate, the greater number of the MSS. treated fall within the fifteenth century, although five of the texts are from the fourteenth, fourteen from the thirteenth, and six are written in what seems to be a hand of the early sixteenth century. Only a few of them — R.3.19 (which belonged to John Stowe, and which contains a goodly number of Lydgate's works), Dd.6.1, and Gg.4.32—appear to be the careful, finished work of professional scribes. From the fact that nearly all the MSS. are Commonplace Books which have passed through the hands of several owners arises the extreme and sometimes bewildering variety of their contents: poetry and prose in English, Latin, and French; long pieces and short scraps; religious and "scientific," devotional and satiric works; riddles and proverbs. In this way the commonplace books reflect only the tastes of their successive owners: in them they copied down, or hired someone else to copy down, whatever seemed useful, artistic, or otherwise worthy of preservation; and in them they tried their own hands at literary composition, especially in margins, on flyleaves, and in such short blank spaces as might be left at the end of some copied selection. This probably accounts for the fact that over half of the poems in the present volume occur in only a single manuscript.

The poems themselves are chiefly lyrical in impulse or form. Many of them reflect the strong religious emphasis of the times; the others serve admirably to exhibit a realistic, questioning, or even a satirical attitude toward certain long-established institutions and a lively, robust sense of humor, equally characteristic of the late Middle English period.

I have tried to reproduce the MS. pages as faithfully as possible "accordyng to my copye and after the symple connynge that god hath lent me." The orthography of the MSS. has been followed throughout. Whenever it has been necessary to introduce emendations to correct obvious scribal blunders the reading of the MS. has been recorded at the foot of the page. Most abbreviations have been expanded. Letters which are omitted in the abbreviations are italicized, but those written in superscript are not. Wherever possible I have been guided in the expansion of abbreviations by the practice of the particular scribe with whose writing I was dealing.

I have carefully studied the scribal lines and markings, describing them when it seemed desirable. At the same time I have refrained from introducing modern punctuation and spelling, believing with Miss Eleanor P. Hammond (*English Verse Between Chaucer and Surrey*, p. ix.) that "while the page may thus lose in clarity for the general reader, it gains greatly for the student, who is then given his proper share in the editorial problem of following the medieval mind. And when examining sentence structure thus, the worker learns far more than when accepting uncritically the conclusions of an editor. Not only can an editor, even the best of editors, hypnotize his readers into false notions of the author's meaning, but the whole subject of Early English punctuation has been slighted and obscured because of such acceptance, continued century after century. We have made it impossible to obtain information on medieval theories of pointing by refusing to print texts with their pointing undisturbed; and the reasons for our refusal are the same as those once considered valid against the reproduction of early spelling—a matter long since settled."

It is hoped that the book, by contributing to the printing of Middle English lyrics, which more than any other form record the attitudes and emotions of those who wrote and those who preserved them, may do its little bit toward shedding light upon a period in the history of our language and our literature that is still not understood nearly as well as it deserves to be. I wish to thank the trustees of the Agnes H. Anderson Research Fund for a grant of assistance; and I am deeply indebted for their whole-hearted encouragement and assistance to the late Professor Dudley D. Griffith and Mr. Joseph Butterworth.

HENRY A. PERSON

April, 1960
Seattle, Washington

CONTENTS

RELIGIOUS POEMS

PRAYERS, SONGS, AND ORISONS TO OR ABOUT GOD, CHRIST, AND THE VIRGIN

An Orison to the Trinity	1
How Sinners Crucify Christ Each Day	3
An ABC Poem on the Passion	5
A Prayer of the Words of Christ on the Cross	6
The Psaltere of Ihesu	8
A Prayer in Memory of the Passion	8
The Wounds of Christ as Remedies Against the Seven Deadly Sins	9
A Second Version	10
Christ Appeals to Man by the Pains of the Passion	11
A Salutacion of Our Lady	11
Ave Maria	14
Heyle, God ye schilde	14
To His Mistress	14
Cur Mundus Militat	16
Translation of *Cur Mundus Militat*	18

PRECEPTS AND ADMONITORY PIECES: SIGNS OF DEATH

Warnings of Death	19

INSTRUCTIVE PIECES: RELIGIOUS, MORAL, RITUAL

The vij vertwys Agyn the vij dedley Synys	21
Augustinus de peccatis venialibus	22
Decem remedia contra peccata venialia ut patebit inferus	23
The Five Goostly Wyttys	24
Lines on the Old Testament Worthies	25
A Riming Exhortation	25
Admonition Against Swearing	26
Health of Body and Soul	26
Penaunce is in Herte Reusing	26

PRAYERS IN ENGLISH RIME

Pater Noster	27
Aue Maria	27
Vii mortalia peccata	27
In eleuacione eucaristie	28
In manus tuas domine	28
In nomine patris	28
Per crucis hoc signum fugiet	28
Mors tua, mors domini &c Vii cogitanda	28
Vestio, cibo, poto, &c Vii opera miserecordie	29

REFLECTIVE (EXEGETICAL) POEMS

On the "Leaps" Which Christ Took   29
On the Value of Prayer and Meditation   30

SECULAR POEMS

LOVE SONGS AND COMPLAINTS

Alas, Alas, and Alas Why   31
Alas What Planet Was I Born Vndir   32
The Lover Wishes His Lady Recovery   32
Lament   33
Without Variance   34
A Troubled Lover's Apostrophe to Death   34
A Compleint vn to Dame Fortune Capitulo xxviii   35
A Pure Balade of Love   38

SATIRICAL PIECES

The Dyscryuyng of a Fayre Lady   38
O Mosy Quince   40
When Women Will Reform   41
Against the Friars and the Fryers Complaynt   41
Punctuation Poem   43
Alas, quid eligam ignoro   44
The Poor Widow and the Rich Man   49

WISE SAYINGS

Exhortation to Study   49
The Vanity of Worldly Lusts   49
The Transitoriness of Worldly Prosperity   50
Of the iiij Complexions   50
Proverbs in Rimed Couplets   52
Praise of Contentment with Little   53

RIDDLES

Aenigmata   53
When I Complain   55
For to Pente   56
THE MANUSCRIPTS   59
NOTES TO THE POEMS   65
APPENDIX   87
BIBLIOGRAPHY   89
INDEX OF FIRST LINES   91

CAMBRIDGE MIDDLE ENGLISH LYRICS

RELIGIOUS POEMS

PRAYERS, SONGS, AND ORISONS TO OR ABOUT GOD, CHRIST, AND THE VIRGIN

1. An Orison to the Trinity

A. Univ. Libr., Ii.6.43, fol. 18r-v.

a llmyȝtty god fadyr of heuen
for cristis loue þat dyde on rode
y prey þe lord to here my steuen
& my desyre fulfyll in god

crist to þy fadir for me praye   5
for hyr loue þat þu lyȝttest [ynne]
& for myȝt grace or þat y dye
me to amende of all my synne

holy [fol. 18v] gost gyf me grace
with suche werkys my lyf to lede   10
þat y may se god in his face
at domis day with oute drede

fadir sone & holy gost
all o god & personis þre·
Almyȝtty god of mercy most·
lord ihesu haue mercy on me· Amen·//

4. MS. fulfyld. *The poem is written as prose, v.2, for instance, beginning
with heuen, and the verso of fol. 18 with gost 9.*

1

B. Univ. Libr., Ii.6.43, fol. 97v.

Oracio deuota de trinitate/ valde bona· /

Lmy3ty god fadyr of heue*n*/
a   ffor c*r*istys loue þat dyed on rode·
·   I p*r*aye þe lorde þou here my steu[en]
A[n]d fulfyᵮ my wyᵮ in goode/·   fol. 98r

Cryst þy fadyr for me praye·   5
ffor hyr*e* loue þou ly3tyst ynne/·
he 3eue me my3t or þat y deye·
Me to ame*n*de of aᵮ my sy*n*ne·

The holygost· þou gra*u*nte me gr*ace*/·
W*ith* suche werk*es* my lyf to lede·   10
þat ·y· maye se god in hys face·
On domes daye w*ith* owten drede/·

Marye þy sone for me þou p*r*aye·
he 3eue me gr*ace* or þat ·y wende·
þat ·y· haue after .y. dye·   15
þe blys of heue*n* w*ith* owten ende·

ffadyr & sone & holygost/·
Aᵮ oo god & p*er*sonys þre
Almy3ti god of my3stes most/·
lorde haue mercy on mee/·   20
And on aᵮ þat m*er*cy nede for charite·//
Ame*n*

C. Univ. Libr., Dd.8.2, fol. 5r.

Almyghty god fader of heuen
for cristes love that deyed yn roode
I p*r*ay the lorde to hire my steven
And my desire cause to be goode

No. 1B: *No stanza division in the MS.; stanzas indicated by double virgules at beginning of lines 5, 9, 13, 17.*
4. MS. goodee.
No. 1C: *No stanza division in MS., but scribal lines indicate stanzas and rime scheme. The page is folded through v. 14.*

To thy fader for me *pray*   5
for here love that thou lightist yn
of myght and *grace* or that I daye
me to amende of al my synne

And *with* suche werkes my lyve to lede
that I may see god yn his face   10
A dovmys day *with* ovten drede
Thorov thy myght helpe and *grace*

ffader sone and holy gooste
One god yn persons three
Almyghty god of mercyes moste   15
And goode lorde haue mercy on me

Mary moder for me pray
that repentance may be yn me
And that I may haue *grace* or þat I daye
Rightfully to amende me   20
      Amen for Cherite

2. How Sinners Crucify Christ Each Day
Caius 174/95, foll. 481-82

Mañ yff thow wylt my mercy gete
Thorough my passioñ of grete vertu
Why sesyst þow me not to bete
Ech day on crosse thow doyst me newe
With thy othys many and gret   5
As a traytor to me thou art ontrewe
And but yf thow wylt thy othes let
Ell*es* full sore hit schall the rewe

No lym of me thou forberyst
Why doyst thow evyll ageynste goode   10
Wyth thy othes þat thou sweryst
fforto a venge thyne veyñ mode

No. 2: *No stanza division in the MS.*

Wyth thy tonge þou me al toteryst
As thou were madde or wode
Wyth thy onkyndnes þou me more deryst   **15**
Thañ they that rent me on the rode

Thow hast more pyte onto thy too
Yf hit be hurt and a lytyll blede
Than thou hast for all the woo
That i suffyrde for thy mysdede   **20**
And whan thou art tauʒt & covñcelyd also
That thou schuldyst not swere but whan hit is nede
A non thou gevyst a scorñ þerto
And to my hestes thou takyst none hede

Loude lesynges for me thou makyst   **25**
Some tyme to wyñ an halpeny
What tyme to wytnesse þou me takyst
And ʒyt thou lyest wetyngly
In byinge & sellyng lesynges þou makyst
And in Idyll and fals thou sweryst me by   **30**
And so to hell the wey thou takyst
Man make amendes or thou dye

Now sore I sygh and wele i may   page 482
ffor i a wrech am so cursyd
That i do the on the crosse ech day   **35**
With grete othys and werkes werst
And moch more the greve than they
That on the rode sloughyñ the fyrst
ffor had they knowe the i dare wele say
To do the to deth they had not dyrst   **40**

But i know it be my beleve
That thou art god omnipotent
And yf i sece not the to greve
I am worthy to be schent
                    Explicit

7. MS. othess (?).   10. *A horizontal stroke runs through* agey/nste.
13. MS. alto teryst.   17. MS. on to
21. *Some letters,* a litt, *crossed out after* &.

3. An ABC Poem on the Passion
Caius Coll., 174/95, p. 482.

Cryste crosse me spede & seynt nycolas
A.b.c. A doth sygnifye
The anguysch that he suffyrd in grete duras
B the blode that he bled so plentyffully
Out of eu*ery* parte of hys deid body   5
C ys the crosse that Judas so tratorly
D ys the dolefull deth of hyɱ so to dye

E eggyng of hys enmyes betokynnyth
ff the fals wytnes of the juys is·
And the gryntyng & the gnascyng þat ys G·   10
*Hij frenduerunt me super dentib*us *suis*
H· ys the harme that they dyd onto hyɱ
J is the Justice that demyd hym to dye
K cowardys of hys dyscypylys fleyng a weye

Wheɱ a yong mayde stode in batayle   15
Oure lady on whoɱ stode the beleve of the
Chyrch yn tyme of passioɱ lo such a vayle·   p. 483
And pr*erogatyfe* women sche dyd wyrch
Sche to an oke but a branche of byrch
Dyd stand & abyde in that grete affray   20
Wheɱ that olde berdyd men dyd fle a way

ȝyt more pr*erogatyf* fell to maɱ
Wheɱ god and man dyed on tre
ffor all mankynde out of hell he waɱ
Onto the place of hye souereynte   25
·L· is the loth lyden in sondre degre
That they made on hym all & some
Saying *crucifige crucifige eum*

·M· the mewys that they made with mockys
Mouentes super eum capita sua   30

5. MS. prte. *Note that p. 483 begins with the rime-word belonging to v. 16.*
21. MS. herdyd.

N· hys nakyd body with wound*es* & knockys
O· the opynnyng of hys hert *cum lancia*
P· the prykkyng of the naylys scharpe & thra
Q· the quakyng of hys body for fere & sory
Quia ex humanite timit mori   35

R· the rubbyng of hys blody clothis
S· the scornes that he dyd thole
T is the tre that hys fals foyes
Dyd hym on to suffer woe
Hys passion hys prayer to the pole   40
Onto hys fad*er* that we my3t rene
With hym the x. y z. and est Ameñ
*Explicit alphabet*um
ffisshar

4. A Prayer of the Words of Christ on the Cross

Univ. Libr., Dd.5.76, p. 1

And as þou wolde c. . . . . en þis wyse
. . . . . þe thefe w*ith* þe in paradyse
Schulde abide w*ith*owten blame
þou grawnte me grace to wirke aƚƚ way
W. . . . hery þat þou may say   5
. . to my sawle þe same

. . d also to þi moder dere
. . . de woma*n* se þi sone es here
. . . . ho was wiƚƚ of rede
And . . . . son þ coryn hey*n*inge   10
Se þar*e* þi moder*e* and w*ith* hir*e* . . . .
Stedfastely in ilk a stede

Grawnt me grace to . . . re . .
And lefe in lofe and charite

No. 4: *There is no stanza division in the MS.*
1. *The* i *in* þis *is inserted above the line.*
10. *The MS. is folded through v. 10.*

Bothe in worde and dede　　　　　　　　15
So þat mari þi modere swete
May be my .. ld my bales to ..
In noyes when I hafe nede

And lorde as þou wol. say hele
And also lamaȝabatani　　　　　　　　20
þat es þus for to say
My god my fadere of mercy fre
W .. has þou forsaken me
. . . .

. . . .　　25
. . . .
. . . .
And þou to wisse synfull wight　　　　p. 2
My lorde my maistere mekil of myght
Als þou with bloid me boght　　　　　30

And as þou sayde greit threst I hafe
þat was man sawle for to safe
ffro dole þat to þaym was dyght
Make me to threst & hafe ȝernyng
þe for to lofe ouer all thyng　　　　　35
With all my mayne and myght

And as þou sayde my sawle I sende
ffadure in to þi holy hende
þat moste es of mercy
þou grawnte me grace to wirke all way　40
Worthely þat I may say
þe wordes whan I schal dy

And as þou sayde at þi nendyng
Ende es now made of all thyng
þat menys þus and no more　　　　　45
Bot þi bales were broght to ende
þe tyme es comen þat þou schall wende
To welthe where þou was ore

þou helpe me lorde þat I may here
.... eit wordes of þi mowthe clere   50
.... my sawle þou þam say
.... my derl ....
....
....

Here saƚƚ þou wone *with* myne Angelis   55
And *with* halous þat in heue*n* dwellis
My kyngedom for to kenne
Lorde lene me grace it may so be
Thorow prayer*e* of þi moder*e* fre
Mayden mari mylde Amen   60

Hic incipit liber de diuersis rebus & medicinis ac vnguentis, etc.

5. The Psaltere of Ihesu

Trin. Coll., O.2.53, fol. 75r.

The Psalter*e* of Jhesu is to sey on the first *pater noster* thies wordys folowyng
Jhesu mercy and graunt mercy
Jhesu for thy mekyƚƚ mercy
As thow art rote and weƚƚ of mercy
So mercyfuƚƚ Jhesu haue mercy on me

And on eue*ry* Ave maria tiƚƚ ye come to the next *pater noster.* Jhesu mercy and so on eue*ry* *pater noster* as it is above and on eue*ry* Ave maria J*hesu* mercy and ther for is grauntyd of pardon a XX yere.*

6. A Prayer in Memory of the Passion

Trin. Coll., O.2.53, fol. 70r.

Thow gracious lord graunt me memory
Eue*r* on thy passion to cry and caƚƚ
Whereby I may the world defye
Whan carnaƚƚ mocions doth on me faƚƚ

*of pard *crossed out after* yere.

Thow blessid Jhesu lord celestyaḻḻ 5
Be thowe defence and me mynd encrece
Thy kyndnesse to remembre and neuer to cesse

7. The Wounds of Christ as Remedies Against the Seven Deadly Sins

Univ. Libr., Mm.4.41, fol. 137v.

Thurwe my ryȝt hande a nayle was driuen
þer on þou think ȝif þou wilt lyuen
And helpe þe pour with almusdede
for I xal ȝelde þe þi mede
Of al my ryche tresour golde & prescius ston 5
þis werld þat is so fiki[1] wil leue me nouȝt on
But a hayre or a schete to hile withal my bon
þerfor I ȝou sey with werdis few
Werldis welth þou hau goday þi leman louis a schrewe
Whayne þou art wroth & wil tak wreche 10
Lok wele þe lore þat I þe teche
Thurw my left honde a nayle he goth
fforȝyf þerfor & be nouȝt wroth
In my ryst vpon þe rode.
Men be me ij thingges þat ware not gode 15
Eysel & gall for to drink.
glotony on þat I rede þou think
Lychour þi lust for me þou lette.
I was for þe boþe boune & bette
To rysin erly þou be nouȝt slowe 20
before þe lyȝt of sunne rysing
ffor gode behechþ þat he xal syng.
A croune to þe þat art walking
Lok my fet hou þay han blede
How þai be nailid to þe tre 25
thanc me þerof it was for þe

No. 6: 6. me *inserted above line.*
No. 7: 3. *The* o *in* pour *is inserted above.*
13. MS. ffor ȝyf.   14. *Harley has* þirst.
21. *The* be *in* before *is inserted above the line.*
23. *The* r *in* croune *is inserted above the line.*

8. A Second Version

Univ. Libr., Ff.5.48, fol. 43v, mid.

MERCY

With a garlande of thornes kene
My hed was crowned & þat was sene   SUPERBIA
The stremes of blode ran be my cheke
þou proude mon lorne to be meke

When þou art wroth & wolde take wreche   5
Kepe wel þe lore þat I þe teche   IRA
Thoro my riȝt hond þe nayle goth
fforgif þerfore and be not wroth

With a spere scharpe and griłł
My hert was woundit with my wiłł   INUIDIA 10
ffor luf of man þat was me dere
Envyous mon of luf þou lere

Rise vp luste out of þi bedde
Thynk on my fete þat ar for bledde   ACCIDIA
And harde nayled vpon a tre   15
Thynk on man þis was for the

Thrugh my right hand þe nayle was driffe
Thynke þer on if þou wilt liffe   AUARICIA
And worshipe god with almysdede
þat at þi deyng heuen may be þi mede   20

In alle my paynes I sufferd on rode   fol. 44r
Man gafe me drynke no thyng gode   GULA
Eysełł and galle for to drynke
Gloton þer on euer þou thynke

Off a mayden I was borne   25
To safe þe folke þat were for lorne   LUXURIA

*No stanza division in the MS. The names of the sins in the margin are
underscored; scribal lines and braces indicate the stanzas.*
14. MS. fote.

Alle my body was beton for syn
Lecchore þer for I rede þe blynne

I was beton for þi sake
Syn þou lefe & schrifte þou take   *IHESUC* 30
ffor sake þi synne and luf me
Amende þe and I forgif þe

9. Christ Appeals to Man by the Pains of the Passion

Trin. Coll., O.2.53, fol. 69r.

O man vnkynde
Haue thow yn mynde
My passyon smert
Thow shall me fynde
To the full kynde   5
Lo here my hert

10. A Salutacion of Our Lady

Univ. Libr., Ff.2.38, fol. 31v.

Here endyþ the seuene salmes & begynneþ a salutacion of oure lady

Heyle fairest þat euyr god fonde
Heyle modyr & mayden free
Heyle floure of Josep wonde
Heyle the fruyt of yesse
Heyle blossome our bale vn bonde   5
Mannes boote was borne of thee
Oure beleeue in the can stonde
Whan cryste was on þe roode tree
Heyle roose on ryse heyle lyllye
Heyle semelyest & swettest sauour   10
Heyle prynces of hygh pytee
Heyle blessyd fruyt swete floure

32. *The next poem begins thus:*
      Herkyns now bothe more and lasse
      I wille yow telle of a heuy casse
No. 9: 1. *Preceded by a crossed-out line in Latin beginning with* Confessio.

Heyle tabernacle þere truþe can telde
Heyle garden þere grasse can spryng   col. 2
Heyle braunche þere blysse can bylde   15
Heyle goodnesse euyr growyng
Heyle youþe þat neuer schaĺ eelde
Heyle bewte euyr dewryng
Heyle scheltrim schouris to shelde
Heyle bryghtnes euyr schynyng   20
Heyle worþy flesche neuyr fadyng
Heyle charytes paramour
Heyle lyfe and lustys lykyng
Heyle blessed mary þat bare þe floure

Heyle quene of heuene blys   25
Heyle lady of þys worlde wyde
Heyle of helle the emparys
Heyle feller of the fendys pryde
Heyle the yoye of blessydnesse
Heyle the welle of heuene wyde   30
Heyle of all aungelys goodnesse
Heyle floure fayre on euery syde.
The desyre þat prophetys can abyde
Heyle systyr of oure senyoure
Pardon þorow whom ys cryedd   35
Heyle fruyt þat bare oure sauyoure

Ryght as the floure fresche of hewe
In fayrenesse passeth with owt wene
So vyrgynes of vertues trewe
Thou passest all that han ben   40
And boþe þe oolde lawe & the newe
In youre selfe they ben seene
Ther was neuer noon þat man knewe
That kepte þem so as y may meene
Heyle day sterre sauyour schene   45
Heyle dere delycyous odoure
Heyle rygall rubyes betweene
Heyle blessyd fruyt swete floure

43. man *is crossed out before* noon.

God hys sone to þe he sende
Wyth heyle mary full of grace   50
Thys worlde may not comprehende
How of thy body bore he was
Heyle medycyne beste may mende   fol. 32r
Heyle comfort to nedy and solas
Heyle tapur that euyr ys/ tende   55
Heyle laumpe þat lyghteneþ in eche place
Heyle fayrest feture of face
Heyle troone of heuene toure
Heyle mercyfull with owt manace
Heyle blessyd fruyt swete floure   60

Heyle olyue heyle vertuouse
Heyle roose with owten any thorne
Heyle grounde moost gracyous
Heyle bryght sonne on somers morne
Heyle goodely glade hayle gloryouse   65
Heyle herte þat with þe swerd was schorne
Heyle Josephs wyfe with thy spouse
Youre owne broþer ye han borne
Was neuyr noon syþen ne beforne
A modur with maydenys honoure   70
Heyle heele to þem þat ben borne
Heyle blessyd fruyt swete floure

Heyle saluyng of seyntys in heuene
Aungels patryerkys and profete
Heyle postlys and martyrs steuene   75
Confessouris and vyrgyns swete
All þat was made in dayes seuene
The honouryþ þankyþ and grete
Whan hyllys and dalys schullen be euene
And body and soule to gedre mete   80
Whan cryste schall schewe hys Woundys Wete
Than marye be oure maynpernoure
That we in heuene mowe haue a sete
And dwelle with the blessyd floure Amen

Here endyþ þe salutacion of oure lady. And begynneþ þe X commaunde-
mentis of almyȝty god   70. MS. Amodur.

11. Ave Maria

Univ. Libr., Gg.4.32, fol. 12r.

Hic incipit salutacio beate virginis marie in eadem lingua

Heil marie ful of wynne·
þe holy gost is þe wiþ inne·
Blesced be þou ouer alle wymmen·
And þe fruit of þin wombe amen·

12. Heyle, God ye schilde

Corpus Christi 405, p. 22.

Heyle god ye schilde / modyr Holy kyng bere milde
Hefne þat in kepyng / haȝ an world wit outyn hondyng
Chaungon hys ryhte Oon kynde sosone michte
þat dede nere synne schuld chyld conseyue vyt ynne
Als sune schene / smyt þour glas wer nis ysenne   5
Wyt outyn tene Wemles bar Child maydyn clene

13. To His Mistress

Trin. Coll., R.3.19, fol. 160v.

Chaucer.

L A D Y of pite for þy sorowes þat þou haddest
ffor Ihesu þy son in tyme of hys passion
haue rewthe of me that ys most maddest
In loue to wryte & shew myn entencion
To her that hath my lyfe in correccion   5
Bothe lyfe & dethe all ys at her wyll
Now helpe me lady & let me nat spyll

Allas howe myght I wryte my souerayn for to plese
Or in what maner to cause her on me rewe
Allas for fere I quake. my hert ys nat at ese   10
My hande doth tremble my ioy ys leyde in mewe
Ther to abyde tyll that my swetyng trewe

No. 12: 2. MS. yat.   4. MS. yat.   5. MS. your.
No. 13: 11. MS. newe.

Me haue relesyd/ but worst ys þat I dowte
That she my payne & labour set at noughte

Most souerayn most sormountyng in goodnes   15
O intemerat Iunyper & daysy delycious
My trust my helthe my cordiall founderes
O medycyne sanatyf my infyrmynat langours
O confortable creature of louers amerous
O excellent herber of louely countenaunce   20
Ye regystre my loue in your remembraunce

My wyt my þought and myne entencion
Ys forto plese yow mastres souerayn
And for your loue þorough many a Region
I wold be exyled so ye wold nat dysdayn   25
To haue pyte on me when I complayn
In wele and wo to suffre perturbaunce
So þat ye wold haue me in remembraunce

My payne ys preuy impossible to dyscerne
My lamentable thoughtes byn cast in mornyng   30
O generall Iuge whyche syttyst superne
Gracyosly graunt me loue of þys mayde ying
O amiable mastres gracious and benygne
I put me holy in your gouernaunce
Exyle me nat out of your remembraunce   35

What myght hit be þat brought me in þys daunce   col. 2
Couetyse or Ryches or byrthe of hygh lynage
Nay nothyng elles safe your womanly contenaunce
Your condicions your maners wyse and sage
Benygne & curteyse thys encreseth your age   40
These virtues reportyd to me & shewyd clere
By oon þat ye know for a curteyse Bachelere.

But mastresse as for my part let þe world wag
I woll nat be yokyd but I coude draw
I haue nat vsyd to bost nor to brag   45

44. w^t *deleted after* yokyd.

Nor false of my worde hit ys no louers law
Wherfore I feyne me & mysylf withdraw
As for a whyle & put yow out of dowt
Though I lak yow yet shall I nat be withowt

Yet for the good wyll þat ye haue me shewyd   50
I wyll do any thyng þat myght yow please
As well as he on whom your loue ys bestowyd
Though hit were to me hurt & gret vnease
But as for your loue. do as yow please
And as for your euyll wyll þerof woll I non   55
ffor hit were ouermoche ij dogges ouer o boon

Now mastresse syth hit ys nat your pleasure
Of loue nolengor to kepe contynuaunce
What noforce go all at auenture
I cannat make stabyll þat ys full of variaunce   60
But oon þyng masteras haue in your rememb[ra]unce
ffor to loue yow I woll do my deueure
And to trust yow whyle my lyfe endure

The Retor Tullius so gay of eloquence
And Ouide that sheweth þe craft of loue expresse   65
With habundaunce of Salomons sapience
And pulcrytude of Absolons fayrenesse
And were possessyd with Iobys gret rychesse
Manly as Sampson my person to auaunce
Yet wold I submyt me in your remembraunce   70
                    Explicit

14. Cur Mundus Militat

Univ. Libr., Mm.4.41, fol. 137r.

Cur mundus militat sub vana gloria
Cuius prosperitas est transitoria
Tam cito labitur eius potentia
Vt uasa figuli que sunt fragilia

There is no stanza division in the MS.
3. MS. sito.   4. MS. fuguli, *with second u inserted above.*

Plus crede literis scriptis in glacie   5
Quam mundi fragilis uane fallacie
ffalax in praemiis virtutis specie
Quis numquam habuit tempus fiducie

Credendum est magis auris fallacibus
Quam mundi misera prosperitatibus   10
ffallcis in sompnis ac vanitatibus
ffalcis in studiis ac voluptatibus

Dic ubi Salomon olim tam nobilis
Vel Samson ubi est dux inuincibilis
Vel pulcher Absolon uultu mirabilis   15
Vel dulcis Ionotas multu amabilis

Quo cesar abiit celsus imperio
Vel diues splendidus totus in prandio
Dic ubi tiulius clarus eloquio
Vel aristotiles summus ingenio   20

Tot clari proceres tot retro spacia
Tot termus praesulum tot regum forcia
Tot mundi principes tanta potencia
In ictu oculi clauduntur omnia

Quam breue festum est haec mundi gloria   25
Vt umbra transiens sunt eius gaudia
Que semper subtrahunt eterna praemia
Et ducunt hominem ad rura diua

Hec carnis gloria que mangnipenditur
Sacris in literis flos feni dicitur   30
Vt lilii folium quod uento rapitur
Sic vita hominis a luce trahitur

O essca vermium o massa pulueris
O ros o vanitas cur sic extolleris

11. MS. j *struck out before* vanitatibus.
15. b *in* Absolon *inserted above.*   32. MS. aluce.

Ingnoras penitus vterum cras uixeris   35
ffac bonum omnibus quam diu poteris   fol. 137v

Nil tuum dixeris quod potes perdere
Quod mundus tribuit intendit rapere
Superna cogita cor sit in ethere
ffelix qui poterit mundums contempnere   40

15. Translation of *Cur Mundus Militat*

Univ. Libr., Mm.4.41, fol. 137 r-v.

þe saule haskis ryȝt as wrytin is in stor[i]e
Qui wil þis werde be knyȝt vnder þe kenges veynglor[i]e
Wos riches & myȝt is cald but transitorie
As vessel of erþe dyȝt so schort is his memorie

Treyst more yf þu be wyse in walkeng of a myle   5
To þe letters wryten in ys þan to þis werdes wyle
In mydis as I am avise disceyuabul is he quyle
Who had euere be held & Ryse trofful teme with gyle

More it sikyr to be . to wyndes þat be fykyle
þan to þis werdes proparte þou it be neuer so mykyle   10
In falce drems & vanite in fleshely lustes tykyle
In coueteyse of grete pouste. þat is þe deuuls prikyle

Say where is keng salamon. þat quilum nobul wace
Or wher is nov fayr absolen. so louely wace in face
Or þe strong duk sampson. for hym men seyne allace   15
þat wer slayne a mong her fon. & swete Ionataas

Whyder is cesar & emperour. so mykel of power
Whider is prince and conquerour. boþe knyȝt & kayser
Tullius þe disputour of speche þat wace so clere
Virgyl þat had no pere   20
Arestotle he bar þe senenȝer til he wace her

No stanza division in the MS.; scribal lines indicate stanzas.
2. MS. þekenges.   5. MS. bewyse.   8. o in trofful inserted above.
17. h in Whyder inserted above.   19. so inserted above.

þus many sshyr lædig*es*. þus many spaes ha gon
Boþe byschop & kyng. of flesche & blode & bon
Dame & dusyper. of hold tyme left non
In a nye tuynkling we xal face eu*e*rikkon   25

Schorte fest made þis werdes blisse : his joys we*n*d son
As þe schadwe þat passande is þ*er*for ma*n* makis mon
Medes lastand w*ith* drawt. I wisse & lettis ma*n*s bon
To wilful feldes lette. o mys þ*er*fore be thy*n*k þe son

As tellis he þat prayet   30
þe flesch so mykel loth*h*ely þat holy wurt vs seyet
As flour of hay he is sothly. as lef of lily þat dyet
W*ith* þe wy*n*d þat blowis forby flyes as foule þat playet
Manns lyf welmore ly3tly : out of his ly3t flyet

A þou flesche þou wurm*es* wast. of pouder a gr*e*te gad*e*ring   35
þou dew þou filth foule of cast. Why makis þou swilk bosting
þou ne wotis for to lyue*n* a blast or dye i*n* þe morning
To all þe my3t þat þou hast do god of werdlithing

Say no thing þat it is þine þat þou maist lesen be ny3t
þe werd wyle raken thurowt þi nyen þat þe 3af or ly3t   40
Think of gode lyfte up þi bryne i*n* to þe heyr so bry3t
Sely wer þat ilk pylgryme þ*is* werde þat haten my3t

In þe space of halua day Wase made þ*is* schorte geste fol. 137v
Ne my3t I te*n*den to swilk play. for sanct Austyns feste
þe Rymis of þe werte aray I hold my beheste   45
old buyst*es* & nou3t gay þat is sen of my cr*e*ste

Precepts and Admonitory Pieces: Signs of Death

16-19. Warnings of Death

Univ. Libr., Ee.4.35, fol. 24r, middle

Whan thy hed quakes *memento*
When they thy leppes blakes *conffessio*

No. 15: 31. MS. lot*e*by. 33. 1 *in* blowis *inserted above line.* 35. MS. agr*e*te.
44. MS. sanstoustyns.

Whan they breyt pantys *contrecio*
Whan they weynde wantys *satisfaxio*
Whan they lymes caldys *libera me domine*   5
Whan they noys kelys than *miserere*
Whan they eyon holowyt *nesse te ipsum*
ffor than deth folwes *Vene Ad Iudecio*m

Univ. Libr., Ff.5.48, fol. 43, top

Memento Homo

When þi hed whaketh/*memento*
When þi lippys blaken/con*fessio*
When thy brest pantis/*contricio*
When þi wynde want*es/satisfactio*
When þi lymmes falys þe/*libera me domine*   5
Nota   When þi nase kelys þen/*miserere*   *bene*
When þine een holoen/*nosce teipsum*
ffor then the deth ffolowes/*Veni ad iudicium*

ihc

Trin. Coll., O.2.53, fol. 72r, bottom

Whan thyn heed shaketh · *memento*
Whan thi lippes quakyth · *Confessio*
Whan thi nose sharpeth · *Contricio*
Whan thi lymmes starketh · *Satisfaccio*
Whan thi brest bantith · *Nosce teipsum*   5
Whan thi wynde wantith *miserere*
Whan thi eighen holoweth · *libera me domine*
Than deth foloweth
Venite ad iudicium

No. 16: 8. *Followed immediately in the same hand without any break in the MS. by scraps of pious proverbial wisdom, e.g.:*
The wrathe of god fforsoyt ys torned into mercey
In a weked sowle shall enter no wesdom yn the body
He that kepys well hes mow*the* & hes tonge he kepyt hes sowle
fro angwysshe.   pro*uerbia.* XXI C°
No. 17:¹1. *The first word of each line is underscored.*
No. 18: 4. s *in* starketh *inserted above.*   6. wynde *written above the line.*

Trin. Coll. B.14. 39, fol. 28r.

Wenne þin eyen beit ihut. & þin heren beoit idut
& list igrauen vndir molde. þu maist ifinden feole vnholde
þat willt striuen afteir þine seluere & þine golde
ant lute þad willt to þine soule ben holde.

INSTRUCTIVE PIECES: RELIGIOUS, MORAL, RITUAL

20. The vij vertwys Agyn the vij dedley Synys

Univ. Libr., Ee.4.35, fol. 5v.

Be meke & meylde yn hert & towng
Ayens pryd boyt olde & yong
Kepe cherite & ffle envey
hate no man yn hert preweley

Suffer thow wronge & cheyde the not   5
Be wer of wreth & veng the not
Be merseyffoll man & thenke where þou art
let mener weres dwell yn they hert

Kepe mesure at met & drynke at melle
ffle gloteney & wet hem not delle   10
Yn clenleynes kepe the chastite & chere
Be thow no lecher yn no menere

Euer werke som werk of honeste
Be neuer ydyll y consell the
These wertwys vij ffle the senys sewyn   15
And then ledyt A man the wey to hewyn

No. 19: 1. MS. eþen.   3, 4. MS. wllit.
*No stanza division in MS., but faultily drawn scribal lines indicate that
a four-line stanza was intended.*
4. MS. prereweley.   13. MS. honest, *before which* ow *is cancelled.*
14. MS. ygyll.   15. senys sewyn.   MS. senysess.

21. Augustinus de peccatis venialibus

Trin. Coll., O.2.40, fol. 103r.

Sepcies in die cadit iustus Perabus 24° Augustinus de peccati; venialibus

1 Fyrst whan a man or a woman drynkes more
  Eny tyme here then myster wore
  Whan þou may helpe thorwgh wytte or skylle
2 And wyl not helpe bot holdes hym stylle
  Whan þou spekes schortly vn to the pore   5
3 That askys som gud at thy dore
  Whan þou art hole & may wele laste
4 And etes wan tyme ware to faste
  Whan þou lyste to slepe & wil not ryse
5 And commes ouer latte in to goddes seruyce   10
  Or whan þou arte in gud state
6 And says thy prears ouer late
  Or whan þou has ouer lytul deuocyon
7 In prears or in orison
  Whan a man wyl dele in bedde   15
  Whyt hys wyfe þat he has wedde
8 Hys lust only to fulfylle
  And to geyt a chylde ys not hys wil
  Whan þou vysyttes men ouer late
  That ys seke in febul state   20
  Or men þat ligges in preson
  Or in angur or in trybulacyon
  Or men þat are synful or sory
  Or soules that are in purgatory
  To vyset them yt ware gret need   25
  Thorowgh praer or thorough almesdede
  Whan þou folowes nouȝth aftur thy state   fol. 103v
  To acord them that are at debate
  Whan þou spekys ouer bytturly
  Vn to any man with noys or cry   30
  Whan þou presys any man more
  Thorowght flateryng than myster wore
  Whan þou in kyrke makys janglyng

MS. braces indicate couplets.   5. t *in* schortly *inserted above.*
21. whan þᵗ *crossed out;* men þᵗ *inserted above.*

Or in wayn thynkys on any thyng
Be yt wit*h*oute be yt wit*h*inne   35
ȝyt yt ys a venial syn
When þou arte lyȝtly worthe
Or sweres & may not holde thyn oythe
Wan þou bannys any man
In whom þou fynd*es* no gylte to banne   40
Whan þou supposys any wyckednese
Thorowgh susspeccyon there no*n* ys
Thyes smale synnys sent austyn tellus
Thorowgh wyche many synnys dwellus
In p*u*rgatory in payn and woo   45
But ȝyt there are many moo
Of venyal synn*es* be many store
Ou*er* thyes þat y haue tolde here before
But so wytte ys no erthly man
That al͛l venyal͛l synnes rekyn can   50
ffor ofte sythes on þe day men falles
In synnes þat clarkes venyal͛l synnes calles
Thorwght thowte or ded or speche i*n* vayn
And yche a syn ys worthy payn

Decem᾿remedia contra peccata venialia, etc.   fol. 104r

22. Decem remedia contra peccata venialia ut patebit inferus

Trin. Coll., O.2.40, fol. 104r.

We fynde wryttyn ·X· thyng*es* sere
That venial synnes for doys here
Theys ·X· are thyes þat I now rede
Holy wat*er* & alm*es* dede
ffastyng and howsyl of godd*es* body   5
Pr*a*er of þe pater n*oster* namely
Seueral schrifte þat yche day may be
Blessyng of bysschop thorough hys dygnyte
And blessyng of preyst þat gyfen ys

No.᾿21: 43. says *is crossed out before* tellus.
No. 22: *MS. braces indicate couplets.*   8. MS. Belssyng, *but cf. v. 9.*

Namely in þe endyng of þe messe 10
Knockyng of brest of man þat ys meke
Laste anoyntyng þat ys gyften to þe seke
Thyes ·X· poyntes puttes veniał synnes away
As men may here thyes clarkes say
But so many veniał synnes sere 15
May be gaderd to gedyr here
That thay may way on þe soule as hewy
As a noder syn ys dedly
That sles þe soule þat god myspays
And therefore þe poyt on thys says 20

De minimis granis fit maxima summa caballo &c

Als of many smale cornes ys mayd
To a hors a gret loyd
Ryȝth so many veniał synnes smale
may make a dedly syn ał

23. The Five Goostly Wyttys

Univ. Libr., Ff.2.38, fol. 32v: col. 1, bottom

Here suen þe ·V· goostly wyttys/
Haue mynde on the blys þat neuer schał blyne
And on grete peyne þat synners shał wynne
Desyre that goddys wylle be wrought
Thy fleschely wylle sett hyt at nought
Rewle the ay be reson ryght 5
And þo þat ben vnder þe aftur þy myght
Vndurstonde goddys kyndenes & hys mercy   col. 2
And ther aȝeyn thyn vnkynde foly
Ymagyne to ał men goodnes/
Ymagyne no wrong nor falsenes/ 10
Of fyue ynwyttys / þe rewle ys thys/
That helpen a man to heuene blys/

Here suen þe VII deedly synnes/

No. 22: 10. of *inserted above the line.*   12. ys *inserted above.*
No. 23: 12. MS. aman.

24. Lines on the Old Testament Worthies

Trin. Coll., B.14.39, fol. 84r.

Iam innocenciam abel audiui. obedienciam habrahe. con-
stanciam. ysaac. tolleranciam Iacob. saltimoniam Ioseph.
iusticiam moysi. misricordiam david. pacienciam Iob.

¶Abel wes looset in treunesse
Habraham in bousumnesse.
Ysaac in studeuestnesse.
Iacob in þinenkenesse.
Ioseph [. . . . .] in edmodnesse   5
& moyses in ritwisnesse.
David þe kinc hede reunesse.
Iob þe gode þolemodnesse.

25. A Riming Exhortation

Univ. Libr., Dd.6.1, fol. 138v.

And ye will please god gretly ·
Use preuey penaunce discretly ·
And deuoute prayers clerly ·
Mesurably eate and drynke ·
Wake praye and thynke ·   5
Be sober sad and chaste ·
And talke no worde in waste ·
As ye love goode mete and drynke ·
So y praye you bothe speke and thynke ·
Loue gentel ihesu feruently ·   10
And take alle aduersyte pacyently ·
And prosperyte mekely ·
And ye schall haue heyvon merely ·
ffor vnder the sunne a man may se ·
Thys worlde ys but a vanyte ·   15
Grace passeth gollde ·
And precyous stoon ·
And god schalbe god ·
When goollde ys goon ·

No. 24: In Latin text, MS. saltimoniam *for sanctimoniam* (?).
5. *A five-letter word has been deleted after* Ioseph.

26. Admonition Against Swearing

Trin. Coll., O.2.53, fol. 66r. (mid)

¶How darest thow swere or be so bold also
To blasfeme hym that is very rote and rynde
And pułł his armes his precious body fro
Alas what vnkendnesse is in thy mynde
Yf thowe were to eny erthly kyng so vnkynde   5
Thow shuldest be drawe and hangyd by þe chyn
As a traytour horrybiłł thogh þou were next of his kyn

27. Health of Body and Soul

Trin. Coll., B.14.39, fol. 42v.

Liuis firist . & licames hele.
þine sinnes heir to beten. & þine soule to saluen
þine children to consailen
& þine frent to gladien
To heowene crist þe sende   5
þer blisse is bouten hende.
God turneþe to þen ilke þinke þat þe is bett to lif
     & to soule.

28. Penaunce is in Herte Reusing

Trin. Coll., B.14.39, fol. 27v: col. 1, bottom, and col. 2, middle

Penaunce is in herte reusinge.
in mouþe tellinge.
in edbote douinge.
for hot. & let euer serwinde.
þou scalt halven heuene at þin endinge.   5
þer is god þat neuer ne lei.
þer is ioye þat neuer [col. 2] ne ageet.

No. 26: 7. *The* a *is inserted above the line after* As.
No. 27: 7. *All the words are in one line in the MS., the writing, as in line 2, getting somewhat smaller toward the end.*
No. 28: 1. *This ten-line poem is written in six lines, four at the bottom of col. 1 and two in the middle of col. 2. The first four lines of the above text are the first two of the MS. Line 5 stands by itself. The column ends with* neuer *7.* *The first of the two lines in col. 2 ends with* Seinte *9.*

þer is lif wid outen deet.
Seinte marie bi sech þi sone.
þat we moten þider com   10

PRAYERS IN ENGLISH RIME

29. Pater Noster

Emmanuel Coll., 27, fol. 162r: col. 1, toward top; col. 2, bottom; 162v.

¶Vre fader in heuene : yhalȝed bo þy name
þy kynedom to us mote come for þar is blisse and game
¶Al þi wille boe ydo : boþe day and niȝt
In heuene also on erthe : alse hit is riȝt
¶Vre euer echedayes bred : þov ȝif vs to day   5
fforgif us vre sunnes : so þov ful wel may
¶Al so wis · so we forgiveþ : here gultes alle
þat aȝen vs helveþ agult : Wov sit bo bifalle
¶Led us neuere Louerd into no fondinge
Ac lus · us · vt of vuele · and ȝif us þy blessinge.   10
¶Amen · / · so mote hit boe ·

30. Aue Maria

¶Heyl boe þov marie : ful of godes grace
God almiȝti is wiþ þe : in eueriche place
Yblessed boe þov Leuedy ouer all wymmen
And þe bled . of þy wombe : blessed boe amen

31. Vii mortalia peccata

¶Prute · ȝisscinge · slevþe · wrethe · and onde :
Glotonie · and lecherie · God bringe hom vt of londe ·

No. 29: 2. come *inserted above.*
5. euer *inserted above.*   10. blessinge *begins line 11.*
No. 31: *The last two words run over into the next line, upon which the title
of No. 32 immediately follows.*

32. In eleuacione eucaristie

¶Wolcome louerd : *in* likninge of bred
ffor me on rode : þat woldest bo deed
Of mine misdede : þov red me red
Schrift and husle : ar ih boe ded
Tiþe me : for þi milsfulhed   5

fol. 162v

33. In manus tuas domine

¶Intoe þine honden louerd : bitech yh gost mi*n*ne
ffor þov me bo3test soþfast god : and luftest vt of sy*n*ne

34. In nomine patris

¶Al fram vuele þinge : me schulde ies*us* þat may
Mid cristes rode tok [n]inge · ih marky · me · today
In þe name of þe fader · and of þe sone · and of þe holigoste ·
Am*en* ·

35. Per crucis hoc signum fugiet

¶Bi þis tokni*n*ge · of þare rode : for f*ra*m me mote floe
Alle wikkedhede : boe wat hit euere boe
And bi þat ulke tokninge : mote boe yborewe
Alle þing þat blessed is : aneu*n*e and amorewe

36. Mors tua, mors domini &c Vii cogitanda

¶Myn o3en deþ and c*ri*stes : and mi wikedhede
Oute of þe dome : and p*ur*gatories drede
þe g*ri*slih pine of helle : and heue*n*iche blisse
Ih o3te to be þenche : ilome bote misse

No. 33: 1. toe *inserted above line.*   MS. bitechyh.
No. 34: 1. eh *crossed out after* fram.

37. Vestio, cibo, poto, &c Vii opera miserecordie

¶Schrude and fede and drenche : and hereborwe þe pouere
Prisones and sikemen : gladien and frofre
Poveris liches burie : after mannes miȝte
þis boþ þe seue [n] workes : þat quemeþ vre driȝte

REFLECTIVE (EXEGETICAL) POEMS

38. On the "Leaps" Which Christ Took

Corp. Christi 294, loose-leaf

Quare velociter ascendit Ihesus tantum spacium in momento . . . .
Also crist steȝ vp hastely . In on stoñde so fer to go
Os.dauid in his prophecy . told be fore hit schuld be so
Exultauit ut gigas ad quendam viam &c
But how fer.he lepe ȝe schyn se . As þe philosophur says here
Raby moyses leue ȝe me . þat writes of hit in þis maner
He says Vij heuenes þer ben . & Vij planetes eke al so   5
& vche planet & heuen be twene . as myche space as mon
    schuld go
Of playne way in .V. hundret ȝere. & space bytwen vchoñ of þo
Os myche space as vche heuon þat is clere. of on wydnes
    beþ boþe two
So þat þe space þat by.twene is . fro heuon to heuoñ as says he
Of as gret wydnes I wys . As is vche of quantyte   10
þen Vij heuones to akount . & Vij spaces hem bytwene
And for to rekoñ wel aryȝt . from myddes of þe vrþe here
to þe hyȝschip & hyȝt of þe seuenþe heuoñ Iii were
þe whyche saturnus called is.Vii þousand hundred & vii space
Os myche as mon schild go I wis . in so long while & he had
    grace   15
Ond to acount vche jorney to fourty myle of euon way
Os vche myle leue ȝe me . two þousant cubytes soþe to say
Ond put al so to vche ȝere iij · hundred days & syxty
þus haue I acounted here. how crist lepte þorow his mercy
to Vij· þousand hit wyl amounte . ȝif þay truly metun ben   20

No. 38: 8. beþ *inserted above the line.*   10. is *inserted above the line.*

39. On the Value of Prayer and Meditation

Trin. Coll., O.1.29, fol. 17v.

¶ffor I wend when any foly me felte.
In þought or speche or any gylte//
þat I sulde in sundyre all ryueñ be.
And kaste from ierusalem my cuntree.//
þat es from heuene þat ilke ricche place.   5
where is all worþe of Ihesu cristes solace
¶I turned me þan vnto my saule euer ilke deele.//
And some comforth I begañ to fele.//
Alle my synnes þai came ryght vnto my þought
¶wylke hadd before tyme caried me to nought   10
¶Of tyme sore þanne I grete and was sorye.//
¶And to a prest of þanne I me schrofe hastelye.//
And þan vnto suet Ihesu I cryede on hie.//
A my lorde Ihesu on me þou haue pite and mersye.
þat for me on þe rode gañ dolefully dye.//   15
Vnto oure lady þan sayde I þus.//
þou praie for me marie to suete Ihesus//
þat he will me gracez gyue to whiles þat y liffe heere.//
To syghe and soroughe for my synnes seere//
So þat þorough his mersie þat y mote wynne   20
¶Onto hym þat sittes aboueñ cherubyn.//
And now mañ þis praiere þat feloughes heere.//
Saye it or þinke it in þi saule þe matere to leere//
ffor whi hym alle tyme þat þe dere bought//
Suld þou in þi mynde haue and in þi þought//   25
And þan salte þou haue forgyfnes of þi foule synne//
And full grete gracez salte þou´fynde þere in
Wylke grace þorough his grete myght//
Sall þe saue bothe day and nyght.// Amen.
¶Explicit liber qui vocatur pupilla oculi etc.

The poem is written as prose in the MS.

SECULAR POEMS

LOVE SONGS AND COMPLAINTS

40. Alas, Alas, and Alas Why

Univ. Libr., Ff.1.6, fol. 137v, middle

Alas alas and alas why
hath fortune done so creweley
ffro me to take awey þe seyte
Of þat þat gewrt my hert lyte

Of aH þyng þat in erth yse   5
To me hyt was þe most blyse
Whan þat y was in presense
To wham my hert doth reuerense

And euer schal for weH or woo   fol. 138r
Or drede of frende or lyf aH soo   10
Hit schal me neuer oþer a sterte
But ye to haue my hole hert

Saue whan I come to þe deth
That nedes oute mouste þe brethe
þat kepyth þe lyfe me with inne   15
And þan fro yow most I twyne

And tyll þe day hit me owre
Ryȝt feythfully I yow ensure
þat þer schal no erly þyng
On my part make departyng   20

Thus ame I sett. yn stable wyse
To lefe and dure in yowre seruyce
Wyt oute faynyng of my hert
Thow I fele neuer soo grete smert

2. e *inserted above line between* l *and* y *in* creweley.

41. Alas What Planet Was I Born Vndir

Univ. Libr., Ff.1.6, fol. 138v.

Alas what planet was y born vndir
My hert ys set thus veray feythfully
Thow y be heuy h*i*t ys no wondir
That in your*e* gr*a*ce y stand not p*er*fetely
Than for to change yet had me leu*er* dy   5
Thes paynes stronge whiche y by force endur*e*
As to loue long y wote y am not sur*e*

And yeff' my dethe come to me hasty
God cnow*t* h*i*t ys by yo*ur* cruelte
H*i*t lith in you al myght ye r*e*medy   10
Of sorow y haue but to grete plente
I fayne no thyng as eu*er* y sauid be
My ioy ys fled' my witt*es* done apeir*e*
I lyue as yet but only in dispeyr*e*

Wher*e* for y p*r*ay as hertly as y can   15
In this grete nede that ye wil me co*m*fort
And thencke y am yo*ur* seruaunt·& yo*ur* man
Els most y for sake al my disport
Wher*e* to bicome or whethir to r*e*sort
Ther ys in me for wo no certaynte   20
ffor lacke of gr*a*ce thes parties shal y flee

42. The Lover Wishes His Lady Recovery

Univ. Libr., Ff.1.6, fol. 28v.

As in yow resstyth my Ioy and co*m*fort
Your*e* dissese ys my mortal payne
Sone god send me seche r*e*porte
þat may co*m*fort myn hert in every vayne
ho but ȝe may me sustayne   5
Ar of my gref be þe r*e*medy
but ye sone ame*n*dement of your*e* maledy

No. 41: 17. a *in* seruaunt *inserted above.*

Weche ys to me þe heviest remembraunce
þat euer can be þouth in any creature
Myne hert hanggyng þus in balaūñce   10
Tyl I haue knowlege & verely sure
þat god in yow hath lyst done thys cure
Of yowre dyssese to haue allygaūñce
And to be releuyd of aħ yowre grevaunce

43. Lament

Univ. Libr., Ff.1.6, fol. 20r, occupying whole page

I may weħ sygh for greuous ys my payne
Now to departe fram yow thys sodenly
My fayre swete hert ye cause me to compleyñ
ffor lacke of yow y stande fuħ pytously
Alle yn dyscomfort withowteñ remedy   5
Most yn my mynde my lady souerayn
Alas for woo departynge hath me slayn

ffare weħ my myrthe & chefe of my comfort
My Ioy ys turnyd ynto heuynesse
Tyħ y agayn to yow may resort   10
As for the tyme y am but recules
lyke to a fygure wyche that ys hertlees
With yow hyt ys god wote y may not fayne
Alas for woo departynge hath me slayne

ʒyt not wythstondynge for aħ my greuaunce   15
Hyt shaħ be taken ryght pacyently
And thenke hit ys to me but a plesaunce
ffor yow to suffre a grete dele more truly
Wyħ neuer change but kepe vnfeyny[n]gly
With alle my myght to be bothe true & playn   20
Alas for woo departynge hath me slayn

17. MS. aplesauñce.   18. ss *is crossed out before* suffre.

44. Without Variance

Univ. Libr., Ff.1.6, fol. 20v.

Margery Hungerford With owte variance
Where y haue chosyn stedefast woħ y be
Newyre to repente in wyħ thowth ne dede
Yow to serue watt ӡe commaund' me
neuer hyt withdrawe for no maner drede
Thus am y bownd by yowre godelyhede   5
Wych haþ me causyd and þat in euery wyse
Wyle I in lyfe endure to do yow my seruyse

Yowre desertt can none odere deserue
Wych ys in my remembrauns both day & nyӡt
Afore al creaturus I yow loue & serue   10
Wyle in thys world I haue streñgth and mytt
Wych ys in dewte of very dewe ryӡt
By promes made with feythful assuraūñcē
Euer yow to sarue with owtyn varyaūñcē

Ye are to blame to sett yowre hert so sore   15
Seþyn þat ye wote that hyt [ys] rekeurles
To encrece yowre payne more & more
Syn þat ye wote þat sche ys merceles

45. A Troubled Lover's Apostrophe to Death

Pembroke Coll. 307, fol. 198v.

O Dethe whylum dysplesant to nature
Where duellyst þow wylte thou þiñ man forsake
Com on and se thow wofuħ creature
That haþᵉ his herte vnto a lady take
That woħ his deþᵉ & lyst no pese to make   5
Cum & helpe the petuys man to ende
In the lythe aħ here ys non odere ffrende

No. 45: 3. on *is written above the line.*   7. *In the blank space intervening
between this poem and the next are several scribblings. The following is legible:*
  . . goode frende
               ⎤ knyghtes
  . . Stanley   ⎦

46. A Compleint vn to Dame Fortune Capitulo xxviii

Univ. Libr., Ff.1.6, fol. 159v.

O þou fortune why art þou so inconstaunt
To make þis land so to meeve
Thou hast a dominacioun traversaunt
Wyth owte numbre doyst þou greeue
Vnstedefast art þou for to be leve   5
He þat yn þe settyth hys confidence
He holdyth ryght naught of clene consciennce

    Radix omnium malorum est cupiditas   fol. 160r
I whoot weel what causyth oure necligennce
fful fewe now þer be content of sufficisaunce
Wherfore þe coveytous doth greet offennce   10
Heygh to surmounte þe worldis bobaunce
Wordely men often tymes hem a vaunce
Be fortune and þat ys here confidennce
he holdyth ryght nawt of clene consciennce

    Qui cupiunt diuites fieri incidunt in laqueos diaboli
Many men byn brought from poverte   15
On to rychesse and þat in dyvers wyse
Whanne þey haue y nough þey cannot se
Poverte þanne doun þey dyspyse
Resoun with hem may not aryse
He þat yn fortune settyth his confidence   20
He kepyth ryght naught of clene conscience

    Multis mortem generauerunt diuitie
Mysure ys tresour as men doon seye
Therto euery man schold take heed
And yn alle his warkes to god obeye
Hym ful hertely loue and dreed   25
And ellys fortune so hym may leed
Puttynge in here al his confidence
A doun to falle in here presence

13. ys *crossed out before* þat.
28. p *crossed out before* here.

Si diuitie vobis affluant nolite cor apponere fol. 160v

Propheta

ffor whanne rychesse doth a bounde
In greet mesure þat ys ful casual 30
fful often tymes yt ys weel founde
þat ful lyghtely · he getyth · a · fal ·
Hys wynnyng at þe last may be smal
In fortune was set hys confidence
He kepte ryght naw3t of clene conscience 35

Manhood in þys reame hath regnyd lange
But now þerfayleth ordynaunce
Covetyse and meede ben had in hand
Sustrys þey be of oon alyaunce
Euery day to gedere þey do daunce 40
3yf men wolde sette in god here confidence
ffare weel þanne large conscience

Coveytyse spredyth now ful wyde
Wherfore worschepe ys set be hynd
Dyscrecioun faylyth now in many a syde 45
Cawsyng rychemen to be blynde
Nyghtes reste can þey noon fynde
In wordely muk ys al here confidence
Therfore absentyth ys clene conscience

ffalseheed ys suster vn to meede 50
Euere þey ben of oon acordaunce
Manye to hem taken good heed fol. 161r
Al þat cawsyth a greet variaunce
Large conscience makyth a dysturbelaunce
In wordely muk ys here confidence 55
ffor þey sette at nawt clene consciennce

That ynfortunat false coveytyse
of gold and syluer falsely gote

29. bund *crossed out before* bounde.
35. kepyth *crossed out before* kepte.
39. MS. a lyaunce.   55. MS. conscidence.

Wher þrough many men doon aryse
And kepyn gold in coferys stoke   60
Day houre and tyme þey ne wote
How long schal endure here confidence
ffor þey sette at nawȝt clene conscience

fful often tymes yt ys y seye
That vntrowthe supportyth tresoun   65
Wher þrought a man may lyghtely deye
ffor falseheed and tresoun ben the enchesoun
In thys land þys mateyr ys not gesoún
Inworldely muk ys his confidence
And al þat causyth · large conscience   70

Holy doctouris thus doon þey seye
That worldely · good gotyn wyth wrong
To resoun þei moste nedys a beye
In helle pette ellys schall þey hong
But restitucioun be mayd among   fol. 161v 75
And trewe repentaunce here defennce
ffor þat wele charyte & clene conscience

Duplex est restitucio scire actualis et mentalis
Restitucion ys weel to vndyrstande
In two wyses as thenkyth me
On · ys þe good þat he hath in hande   80
To ȝeelde yt ageyn to hys powste
That other ys þe good spendyd in vanyte
Good wyl to ȝeelde yt with owte vyolence
ffor þat wele charyte and conscience

Coveytyse dooth often ful greet schame   85
Vnto manhood and þat ys greet pyte
ffalseheed þerof beryth þe name
And þat ys for lak of charyte
Thus many men faren of euery degre

59. may *crossed out before* many.
63. navt *crossed out before* nawȝt.
66. dye *crossed out before* deye.
76. *The medial* e *in* trewe *is inserted above the line.*

In worldely muk lyeth here confidence   90
And al þis causyth large conscience

Nemo potest duobus dominis seruire contrarijs
He þat ys servaunt vn to greet rychesse
And wyl not governe yt to goddys intent
That may lette hym from goddys presence
And so par aventure he may be schent   95

47. A Pure Balade of Love

Caius Coll. 176, fol. 23r, top

Kny3tes in travayle for to serve
Wherof the may thanke deserve
Where as thes men of Armes be
Some most ouer the gret see
So that by lande and by shī͞p   5
The most travayle for wurshī͞p
And make many hasty rodes
Somtyme Vnto ynde sumtyme to þᵉ Rodes
And somtyme in to tartary
So that the herialte on theym crye   10
Viallant viallant Lo where he goith
And then he gyvith hym gold & cloth

SATIRICAL PIECES

48. The Dyscryuyng of a Fayre Lady

Trin. Coll., R.3.19, fol. 205r.

I HAUE a Lady where so she be   by Chaucer.
That seldom ys the souerayñ of my thought
On whos beawte when I beholde and se
Remembryng me how welł she ys wrought
I thanke fortune that to hyr grace me brought   5

No. 47: 12. *This poem is followed by "A Nother balade," vv. 1-14 of Chaucer's Purse, printed by MacCracken, MLN, XXVII, 228f.*

So fayre ys she but nothyng angelyke
Hyr bewty ys to none other lyke.

ffor hardely and she were made of brasse
fface and all she hath y nowgh fayrenesse
hyr eyen byn holow and grene as any grasse   10
And rauynnysshe yelow ys hyr sonny tresse
Therto she hath of euery comlynesse
Suche quantyte yeuyn hyr by nature
That with the leest she ys of hyr stature

And as a bolt hyr browes byn y bent   15
And byttyll browyd she ys also with all
And of hir wytte as sympyll and innocent
As ys a chylde that can no good at all
She ys nat thyk hyr stature ys but small
Hyr fyngers byn lytyll and nothyng long   20
Hyr skyñ ys smothe as any oxys tong

Therto she ys so wyse in dalyaunce
And besette hyr wordes so womanly
That hyr to here hit doth me dysplesaunce
ffor that she seyth ys sayde so connyngly   25
Then when that ther' be mo then she & I
I had leuer she were of talkyng styll
Then that she shuld so goodly speche spyll

And slowth noone shall haue in her' entresse
So dylygent ys she and virtulesse   30
And so besy ay all good to vndresse
That as a she ape she ys harmelesse
And as an hornet meke and pytelesse
With that she ys so wyse and circumspecte
That prudent nooñ hyr foly can infecte   35

Ys hit nat ioy that suche oone of hyr age   fol. 205v
Withyn the boundys of so gret tendyrnesse
Shuld in her werke be so sad and sage

15. MS. hys.

That of the weddyng sawe aꝉ the noblesse
Of quene Jane and was tho as I gesse   40
But of the age of yeres X and fyue
I trow ther ar nat many suche alyue

ffor as Jhesu my synfuꝉ sowle saue
There nys creature in aꝉ thys world lyuyng
Lyke vnto hyr that I wold gladly haue   45
So pleseth myñ hert that goodly swete thyng
Whos sowle in haste vnto hys blysse bryng
That furst hyr formyd to be a creature
ffor were she wele of me I dyd no cure
      Explicit the Dyscryuyng of a fayre lady

49. O Mosy Quince

Trin. Coll., R.3.19, fol. 205v.

Chaucer. O mosy Quince hangyng by your′ stalke
The whyche noman dar′ pluk away ner take
Of aꝉ the folk that passe forby or walke
Your′ flowres fresshe be fallyn away and shake
I am ryght sory masteras for your sake   5
Ye seme a thyng that aꝉ men haue forgotyn
Ye be so rype ye wex almost rotyn

Wyne women worshyp vnweldy age
Make men to fonne for lak in theyr′ resons
Elde causeth dulnesse and dotage   10
And worshyp chaunge of condicions
Excesse of wyne blyndeth theyr′ dyscrecions
And aꝉ bookes that poetes made & radde
Seyen women most make men madde

Your′ vgly chere deynous & froward   15
Your′ grene eyen frownyng and nat glad
Yowre chekes enbonyd lyke a melow costard
Colour of Orenge your brestys satournad
Gylt opon warantyse the colour wyꝉ nat fade

Bawsyn buttockyd belyed lyke a tonne   20
Men cry seynt Barbara at lowsyng of yo*ur* gonne

My louely lewde masterasse take consideracion   fol. 206r
I am so sorowfu⊬ there as ye be absent
The flowre of the barkfate þe fowlyst of a⊬ the nacion
To loue yow but a lyty⊬ hit myne entent   25
The swert hath y swent yow the smoke hath yow shent
I trowe ye haue be layde opon som kylne to dry
Ye do me so moche worshyp there as ye be p*r*esent
Of a⊬ wemen I loue yow best . a thowsand tymes fy.
Explicit

50. When Women Will Reform
Univ. Libr., Gg.4.12, last flyleaf

*Didiscere flere feminam mendaciu*m *est*
When fishes in the water leve their swymmyng
And the byrd*es* in the wood*es* their syngyng
Then the craftie women desist their wepyng
Deludyng their sely husband*es* by fals lyng

51. Against the Friars and the Fryers Complaynt
St. John's Coll. G. 28, flyleaf

þou þat sellest þe worde of god
Be þou berfot be þou schod
    Cu*m* neuer*e* her*e*
*In pr*inci*pio erat verbu*m
Is þe worde of god alle & su*m*   5
    þat þou sellest lewed frer*e*

Hit is cursed symonie
E*þer* to selle or to bÿe
    Ony gostly þinge
*þerf*ore frer*e* go as þou come   10
& hold þe i*n* þi hows at home
    til we þe almis brynge

No. 50: 3. *In margin:* "*John Campyne⊬*."

Goddis lawe ȝe reuerson
And mennes howsis ȝe presen
　As poul beriþ wittnes　　　　　　　15
As mÿddaÿ deuelis goynge abowte
for moneÿ lowle ȝe lowte
　flatteringe boyth more & lesse

The Fryers Complaynt

¶Allas what schul we freris do
Now lewed men kun holy writ
Alle abowte wherre I go
þei aposen me of it

þen wondriþ me þat it is so　　　　　5
how lewed men kan alle wite
Sertenly we be vn do
But if we mo amende it

I trowe þe deuel browȝt it aboute
To write þe gospel in englishe　　　10
ffor lewed men ben nowe so stowt
þat þei ȝeuen vs neyþer fleche ne fishe

When I come in to a schope
for to say *in principio*
þei bidine me goo forþ lewed poppe　15
& worche & win my siluer so

Yf Y sae hit longoþ not
ffor prestis to worche where þei go
þei leggen for hem holi writ
And sein þat seint polle did soo　　　20

þan þei loken on my nabete
& sein forsoþe withoutton oþes

18. flaterynge *crossed out and* flatteringe *inserted above line.*
The Fryers Complaynt *in margin in a later hand.*
14. MS. forto, inprincipio.

Wheþer it be russet black or white
It is worþe alle oure werynge cloþes

I seye I not for me   25
bot for them þat haue none
þei seyne þou hauist to or þre
ȝeue hem þat nedith þerof oone

þus oure disseytis bene aspiede
In þis maner & mani moo   30
fewe men bedden vs abyde
but heyfast þat we were goo

If it goo forþe in þis maner
It wole doen vs myche gyle
Men schul fynde vnneþe a frere   35
In englonde wiþin a whille

52. Punctuation Poem

Pembroke Coll. 307, fol. 197v.

Trvsty · seldom/ to their ffrendys vniust·/
Gladd for to helpp · no Crysten creator/
Wyllyng to greve · settyng all þeir ioy & lust
Only in þe pleasour of god · Havyng no cure/
Who is most ryche · With them þey wylbe sewer/   5
Wher nede is · gevyng neyther reward ne ffee/
Vnresonably · Thus lyve prestys · parde·/

Trusty · seldom / to ther ffrendys vniust ·
Glade for to helpe · no Cristen creator   9
Willyng to greue · settyng all ther ioy & lust   Johan
Only in þe pleasour of gode · Havyng no cure   Mundy
Who is most ryche · with them þei wilbe sure
Wher nede is · gewyng nether rewarde ne ffee
Vnresonably. Thus leve prestys parde

No. 51: 23. blak *crossed out;* black *inserted above line.*
26. them *inserted above line.*
No. 52: 3. *In* þeir, *the* ir *is written in above the* e.

53. Alas, quid eligam ignoro

Univ. Libr., Hh.4.12, fol. 91r.

Consideryñg effectually the gret diuersite
Of sectys conteynyd in the church present
How eche of hem lyve in a dew degre
Presthode and religioñ euer to be continent
The layfee in sposayłł/ the solitary doth consent   5
Euer to be contemplatyf/ we se wełł it is so
Wherefore thus I said verayly as I ment
Alas/*Quid eligam ignoro*

¶Thre thyngges quod Salamon ben vnknowyn to me
And to know the fowrth I can not vtterly   10
The way of shypp saylyng in the see
The way of an heddyr glydyng sodayly
Of the egle in the ayere the way is fułł slye
The worst of ałł to know is of a yong man loo
Wherefore thus I said sore syghyng inwarly   15
Alas *Quid eligam ignoro*   fol. 91v

¶ffor whan I was determined fyrst to go to scole
It was to me ryght lothe by cause of castigacion
ȝit me thowght ageynward elles shuld I be a fole
Wich to ałł my frendes shuld be diffamacion   20
Thus toward and froward I had persuasion
Vtterly vnknowyng the best for me to do
Wherefore thus I said havyng noo consolacion
Alas *Quid eligam ignoro*

¶Yit as my fortune wold I was set to lore   25
And growndly in gramer had congrue vndirstondyng
ffurther to procede than set I lityłł store
Thynkkyng myself able to purchase my lyvyng
Yit in my consaite I was ymaginyng
If I forth procede muche better shuld I doo   30
Wherefore thus I said of thys mater musyng
Alas / *Quid eligam ignoro*

15. ly *crossed out after* syghyng.
21. persecucion *crossed out before* persuasion.   25. MS. wat.

¶Thys yit not wi*th*stondyng wi*th* a good avise
My frend*es* me told it is thy furtheraunce
To lerne the ·Vij· science replenyschyd wi*th* delite   35
Yit me thowght to lucre they shuld me nowt avance
And to be a Ciuilistre is a full hard chaunce
Bok*es* be so dere I know well it is so
Wherefore sore complaynyng thys was my daliance
Alas / *Quid eligam ignoro*   40

¶Than happyd that in arte I had the magistery
My Regency finischyd I had habilite
ffurther to procede I wold no leng*er* tary
to ffysyk or to Ciuille was my felicite
But whed*er* of them both had more affinite   45
To iust adquisic*i*on I cowde not chese thoo
Wherefore thus I said in that aduersite
Alas / *Quid eligam ignoro/*

¶Than thowght I forto be in spirituall lawe   fol. 92r
An officiall / aduocat / procto*ur* / or notary   50
Anone I was counsellyd thens me to wi*th*draw
Lest I shuld misuse the law / wich wold not varye
Thus mouyd vnwarly I gan both banne and wary
Like vnto a Reede wavyng too and fro
Wherefor*e* thus I said I cowd no leng*er* tarye   55
Alas / *Quid eligam ignoro.*

¶Wel I wote thatt Canon and holy theologie
Ben best of all other mannys sowle to co*n*uay
All heresy confoundyng and fals Ipocrisye
Them wold I haf lernyd the soth for to sey   60
My fraylte me com*m*andyd not for clymme so hye
Lest I beyng there sodaynly fall hem fro
Wherefor thus I said seyng non othyr way
Alas *Quid eligam ignoro/*

¶Thus mortally bewavyd wi*th* stormys procellows   65
I nyst where to fynd the porte of stedfastnesse

65. MS. *bewavys.*

To which I myght we*ll* guye my lyfe thus trobelows
ffor if I were a prest su*m* men wold than gesse
That I so dyd for couetyse of ease and sikyrnesse
Agayneward if I weddyd war than shuld I lefe in woo   70
Wherfor thus I said havyng gret heuynesse
Alas *Quid eligam ignoro*

¶The mownte of co*n*templac*i*on strong it is to stey
Inhabited w*ith* possessioner and w*ith* mendinant
If I be a frere I may begge alway   75
Many diu*er*se townys frely for to hawnt
Yf I be possessioner I haf noo such grawnt
ffor I must lyffe in cloystre wheder I wyl or noo
Wherfor thus I sayd in wytte a yong enfawnt
Alas *Quid eligam ignoro*   80

¶Whan I had thus co*m*playnyd exp*re*ssyng myn entent fol. 92v
A yong man herd my p*r*ocesse disposyd worldly
O me*r*cy god qu*od* he now am I but shent
Sith thys wyse clerk co*m*playnyth so vttirly
what is best to doo / not knowyng v*er*ayly   85
And in worldly besinesse is most trobles woo
Wherfor thus I say grett*er* cause haf I
Alas / *Quid eligam ignoro*/

¶A man to be a marchaunt he said was aventure
Of body and good*es* hit is trowth in dede   90
Of shipwrak and piratys hard is the recure
To dyeke or to delue he wold for no nede
To begge hym thowght shame so god hym spede
Of theys to chese the lest was payne and woo
Wherfor*e* thus he said I toke to hym good hede   95
Alas *Quid eligam ignoro*

¶In cowrt to be bownde to dew attendaunce
Or to be in office myght torne to hys avayle   [marg.:
Yit hym thowght agayneward ther myght hap a cha   unce]
That as an vngiltles innocent he shuld be put in gayle 100
As Ioseph was and danie*ll* that is w*ith* owt faile
89. MS. Aman.   100. be *inserted above line.*

And for to gete hys lyvyng sumwhat must he do
Wherfor thus he said and gan both wepe and waile
Alas *Quid eligam ignoro*

¶To lerne the lawe temporall grete goodes myght he gete   **10S**
As to be in the chauncery or theschequire
Aftyr to be sargēāñt causys for to plete
Which gettyng as hym thowght was not inly clere
Accordyng with hys conscience which shuld be the stere
Of thys wrechyd lyvyng yf we shall well doo   **110**
Wherfor he said with ryght a piteuowse chere
Alas / *Quid eligam ignoro*

¶To be an hand crafty man must hafe gret besinesse   fol. 93r
As to be a tailyour wryghte / or coteler
And dayly now in craftys is falshode and dowblenesse   **115**
Therfor to þis yong man in noo wyse they were dere
And vttyrly he forsoke to be a laborere
As to dawbe or dyke he myght not swynk soo
Wherfor thus he said standyng in grete dwere
Alas *Quid eligam ignoro*   **120**

¶In any wyse he said I will haf a wyfe
Shall I wed the bewteuose nay quod jelosye
I wyll not wed the fowle for irkyng of my lyfe
The ryche be passyng strawnge the good ryght rare to spie
To parell with the jentyll I may not clymbe soo hye   **125**
And if I wed a chrewe my good days than be doo
Wherfor thus he said as lowde as he myght crye
Alas *Quid eligam ignoro*

¶Thys piteuows gret complaynt of thys yong persone
Vggyd so myn erys my tounge cowd not refrayne   **130**
To say on thys wyse yong man leve thy mone
The mater that thow waylist towchith both us twayne
And thow we be now lokkyd with one woful chayne
Yit we may haf remedy expellyng all owre woo
Neuer sayng aftyr / as we wer wont to sayne   **135**
Alas *Quid eligam ignoro*

¶Lat us take ensample of wofull susanne
By duresse put to dye / orto consent to synne
Synne yit she ne wyll / for noo powere of man
But rather chese to dye by fore all hyr kynne   140
The peple sorowyd sore both more and mynne
Yit god thorow hys grace deliuerd hyr fro woo
So may he do us to say than may we blynne
Alas *Quid Eligam ignoro*   fol. 93v

¶Beseche we now for grace the lord omnipotent   145
That we may chese the way most to hys plesaunce
Whos grace to saint powle was so sufficient
That of hys gostly enmys he had no noyance
What nedith rehersall of Grisild or Custaunce
Preseruyd thorow grace and othyr many moo   150
We shall trust in god voydyng thys daliaunce
Alas *Quid eligam ignoro*

¶Who made the so hardy thow simple balad
The presence to approche of poetys lawreate
With robys of rethoryk sith thow art not clad   155
But with rusty roset like to thyn astate
Of homly boystyrs langage most rude and desolate
Make therfor thys excuse in place which thow commyst
I wyll neuer reherse thys clause disconsolate
Alas *Quid eligam ignoro*   160

Eke say to thyn excuse I were upon my bake
The first mysshape cote of vnpullischyd speche
That euer my maister made whos colour is ryght blak
To dye with tungges purpurat wold god ʒe wold hym teche
Which hygh abofe the sterrys in rethoryk doun areche   165
That I myght ben arayed like the gloriose poo
Than durst I be ryght bold thys refreyt for to preche
Alas *Quid eligam ignoro*
                    Explicit

154. *The second* a *of* lawreate *is above the line.*
·156. who *in margin.*   165. MS. a bofe, a reche.

54. The Poor Widow and the Rich Man

Trin. Coll., B.14.39, fol. 28r.

A vidue pouere was. & freo
& luttel lond held heo.
A riche hurede tre false widnesse
Of sale to tellen sikyrnesse
So ic mote to day aueder*es*   5
& firbernen Wid al mine weder*es*
þe riche boute enne aker of lond:
& payede þe widue hond of hond·
þe oþer þer fel i*n* parlesie·
þe þirde firbraid ful witerlie·   10

WISE SAYINGS

55. Exhortation to Study

Trin. Coll., O.2.53, fol. 60r.

Enforce thy wytt*es* for to lere
Aquaynt the wyth connyng for it is sure
yf fortune chaunge and pou*er*te a pere
He that ys connyng ys lyke to recure

56. The Vanity of Worldly Lusts

Trin. Coll., O.2.53, fol. 73v.

What helpith it man to be vnstable
To sett his p*re*sent lust on worldly vanyte
Syth aƚƚ the Joy þerof is t*r*ansmutable
Beaute rychesse strength and p*ro*sp*er*yte
Trust ryght weƚƚ aƚƚ these shalle from þᵉ fle   5
Save dedys good & badd payn or blysse
It shaƚƚ not noy þᵉ ofte to thynk on this

No. 54: 10. MS. þrirde.

57. The Transitoriness of Worldly Prosperity

Trin. Coll., R.3.19, fol. 67r.

The vnware woo that commeth on gladnesse
Ys vnto hertys passyng encomberouse
And who hathe felte hys part of wylfulnesse
Sorow sewyng on ys to hym odiouse
And worst of aH and most contrariouse   5
Ys when the statys hyghest of renowne
Byn from theyre noblesse sodenly brought downe

Vacat Bettyr ys to dy then euer to lyue in peyne   *Vacat*
Bettyr ys an ende then dedely heuynesse
Bettyr ys to dy then euer in woo compleyne   10
Bettyr ys to dy then lyue in wrechydnesse
And where as myschyef doth at foHk dysdeyne
By wofuH constreynte of long contynuaunce
Bettyr ys to dy then lyue in suche penaunce

58. Of the iiij Complexions

Trin. Coll., R.3.19, fol. 52v.

Sanguineus *Natura pingues isti sunt atque forantes*
Atque rumores cupiunt audire frequenter
Hos venis & brachijs delectant fercula risus
Et facit hos hillares et dulcea verba loquentes
Omnibus hij studiis habiles sunt ac magis apti   5
Qualibet ex causa nec hos leuiter mouet Ira
Largus amans hillaris ridens Rubri que coloris
Cantans carnosus satis audax atque benignus

Of yiftis large in love hathe gret delite
Jocond and glad ay of lawyng chere   10
Of Ruddy coloure meynt somdel with whight
Disposud be kynd to be a chauntere
Hardy I nowe manly and bold of chere
Of the Sanguine also it is a signe
To be demur Riche curteys and benigne   15

Colericus   *Est humor colere qui conuenit impetuoso*
                 Nam genus hominum cupiunt percellere cunctos
                 Hij leuiter discunt multum comedunt cito crescunt
                 Ideo magnanimi sunt magni summa petentes
                 Hircutus fallax Irascens perditus audax   20

                 The coleric froward and full of disceyt
                 Irous in hert prodiggall in expence
                 Hardy also and werchithe ay be sleight
                 Slender and smal full light in existens
                 Right drye of nature for the gret fervens   25
                 of het and the Coleric hathe this signe
                 He is comonly of coloure Citryne

fflegmaticus *fflegma viros modicos latos faciet quoque*
                          breves   fol. 53r
                 fflegma facit pingues sanguis reddit mediocres
                 Otio non studio tradunt se corpora sompno
                 Sensus hebes terdus motus pigrina sompnus
                 Hic sompnolentus piger in sputamine multus

                 The flewmatique is sompnolent and slowe
                 With humores grosse replete ay habundaunt
                 To spitte Inuenons the fleumatic is knowe 35
                 By dull conseyt and voide vnsuffisaunt
                 The suptill art to accomplissh or haunt
                 ffat of kynd the flewmous men may trace
                 And know them best be fatnes of ther face

Malencolicus *Restat ad huc tristis colore substancia nigro* 40
                 Que reddit tristes paruos que pauca loquentes
                 Hii vigilant studio nec mens est dedita sompno
                 Servant propositum sibi nil reputant fore tutum
                 Inuidus et cupidus tristis dextre que tenacis

                 The malancolius thus men aspie   45
                 He is thoughtful and set in coviteys

22, 35. Irous, Inuenons. *Robbins' readings from Harley MS.*, Sec. Lyr. XIV and XV Cent., *p. 72.*   31. MS. ebes.

Replenysshed full of fretyng Envie
Hes hert servithe hym to spend in no wise
Treason Envious fraude can he well devise
Coward of kynd when he shuld be a man   50
Thou shalt hym knowe be visage pale & wan
Explicit iiij complexions

59. Proverbs in Rimed Couplets

Trin. Coll., O.9.38, fol. 70r.

¶Salamon seyth ther iş none accorde
Ther eu*ery* man wuld be a lord
¶Wher eu*ery* man is plesyd w*ith* his degre
Ther is both pece and vnyte
¶Whos consciens is combred and is not clene   5
Of other men dedis the wursse wull deme
¶Deme not my dedys thowgh thyne be nowght
deme what þou wult . þou knowist not my thowghte
¶Demyng' and mvsyng' over ferre
Meny mennys wyttys it settisse yn erre   10
¶Power possessyon and rychesse
No man may sette yn sykernesse
¶The ende of lust is sorow and schame
Travell and parell and lost of name
¶loue to amende . and feyne to please   15
lothe to defende sufferaunce doth ease
¶In eu*ery* place wher y gan fare
lacke of forwytte is cause of care
¶Thow hast noo charter of thy lyfe
Cause þou neu*er* bate nother stryfe   20
¶Be neu*er* thrall vn to synne
And thynke on þe ende or þou be gynne
¶Ouer thy hed loke þou neu*er* hew
Pou*er*te hath but frendys few
¶Who so of welth takith no hede   25
He schall fynde fawte yn tyme of hede

10. sett *is crossed out before* settisse.   18. MS. for wytte.

¶Thys worlde is mvtabyłł so seyth sage
Therfor gedyr yn tyme · or thow fałł yn age
¶Grace passyth golde and precyous stone
God schałł be god when golde is gone

60. Praise of Contentment with Little

Univ. Libr., Gg.4.12, last flyleaf

Tuta paupertas
Hiegh Towers by strong wynd*es* fułł lowe be cast
When the lowe Cotages stand sure & fast
Therfor w*ith* surenes yt is bett*er* in povertie tabide
Then hastily to be Riche and sodaynly to slyde

RIDDLES

Univ. Libr., Dd.5.76, flyleaf opposite p. 1

Aenigmata

61

Ther was a ladie leaned her backe to a wall
  He tokke vppe peticote smokke & all
  He laid her legg*es* vppon his knee   A shoon
  It was̓ a[s] white as white might bee
  He took a thing that stiffe did stand   5
  & hunched her & punched her & made great game
O god*es* bodie says she fie for shame
Yet he would not leave her so
But he did ease her & please her befor he would goo

62

Two stones hathe yt or els yt is wrong
  with a bald hed & a tag somwhat long

No. 61: 9. MS. did *is written in above* would, *which has been crossed out.*

& in the night when women lie awake   A clocke
wit ther conscience they doe yt take

63

I haue a hole aboue my knee
& pricked yt was & pricked shalbe
& yet yt is not sore   sheath
& yet yt shalbe pricked more

64

I haue a thing and roughe yt is
   & *in* th[e] middest a hole ther is
Ther cam a ʒong man with his gin   a gloue
& thrust yt even a handfull in

65

Backe bent smocke rent
   Slipperie yt was & in yt went
Thrust in stiffe standing   a test [?]
   But comes out lither dropping
Stiff standing roughe handling   5
   Between a womans legges in a morning

66

Ther ys a thyng as I suppose
W*hi*ch hath a face but never a nose
hath a mouthe but no toth therin   a placht
hath a bearde but never a chin

No. 64: line 1. a *written above line.*
No. 65: line 5. MS. standinging. *Indentation in this stanza is quite
irregular.* Stiff *and* Between *are written above the line. There is no space
between the riddles except for a gap between Nos. 62 and 63. No. 66 is written
in the space to the right of Nos. 64 and 65.*

67. When I Complain

Trin. Coll., B.2.18, fol. 100r.

And' Y com[pleyne]

Whane I compley[n]e
ther is no Resone
yet incertayne
all owte of seasone
to make my mone ·
ther is my most co*m*forte
to lyue alone ·
ther I resorte
to rufullnes ·
for my solas   5
then may ye gesse
wher eu*er* I pas
no worly myrth ·
to my pore hart
for in my birth ·
ther is my smirte
for su*m*tyme I ·
with Jokone spryte
how can deny ·
truly ded sytte   10
eu*er* as I wold
in myrth & playe
as thowght ho shold
then saye me naye
but on a tyme ·
Resone me abassyd'
as a deuyne
my corage dassyd'
my byrth holy
when he declaryd'   15
to leue foly
on me he daryd'
with cou*n*tenance
of rufull chere
maky*ng* se*m*blance
soberly dyd apere
& said my fre*n*de
quyckly I the adwyse
marke the end
for so do me*n* wise   20
that loue gostly
after the sely sole
& not bostly
to turne ther the bole
the bredare ay
of gloteny in dede
when deth repaye
then ther is no spede
of my felowe
that callyd is grace   25
but to lowt low
with avha*n* & dedly face
& passith yᵉ sprite
to his lyke vsage
for ther no wyt
the nowghty abvsage
may then excuse
in that strange passage
thowghe he refuse
what that grete outrage   30

4. *I take syche coortte is crossed out and* ther wher that I resorte *is written in the line below, with* wher that *crossed out. In the left column there is a space between vv. 4 and 5.*

20. *In the space between vv. 20 and 21 that* make *is written in the left column and then crossed out.*   24a. MS. dethrepaye.

30. grete *is written above* myghty, *and the latter is crossed out.*

a byrth truly

coniecture I

spryte & body

as I dyd aspy

with doful face

tryppyd in trace

as thinges in smert

o pore then hart

to spend pondes

for so redondes

of mysery

thyne enemy

the folle couey

for abvsiggayne sey

whyche very god

    Set heyer

by example

saing a man

the tell howe can

to yᵉ plesure

wher no tresure

in custody

how ca[n] deny

to his euer

aye reuers

in blasfemyng

that very departing

as thowght a martyng

then departe in twene

admyxid with sore payne

in maner of couert wise   35

of a late devyse

only for that deceuer

truly ther is no leuer

    fol. 100v

frendes other ther to make

the sowne of dedly lake   40

in this wrechyd lyffe

then is ther all ryfe

will he to derknes

of thy gret goodnes

hath well showyd the   45

    at on hyl

hangyng on ye tre

what alith the nowe

mekely how I ded bowe

of god my father

then had me rather   50

but euer dyd apply

my hole will truly

in all maner of poyntes

of my tender Joyntes

by this cursyd othis   55

68. For to Pente

Univ. Libr., Ff.1.6, foll. 143v-144r.

ffor to peñte   hyt were ffoly

And after rep[e]ñte

34. *The first letter of the second column is a cancelled* w.

37. only *is written above the line and to the left in the margin of the second column. This margin is fairly regular, but, of course, not as regular as the above copy would indicate.*   46. MS. lyl.

55. MS. *of by,* with *of crossed out. The following* this *is written above the line.*

No. 68: *Scribal lines join the short couplets in the lefthand column.*

1. *Index emends to* p[reue]nte.

Other wass then troyth
me wer ffull loyth
    trewly

I sweyte ffor ffeñte
leste I be scheñt
    To a pere

The rememberauns
Off my plesauns
    Compyled here

Off a starre
Wyth owte cõparre
    Be lykenesse   5

In the beyme
That hyt ys En
    most off swettnesse

And more orryauñd
And pwere gloryaund
    In bewte

Off all othere
hyt ys the modere
    In myn ee

In a cloud off blewe
hyt Dyd never remewe
    The spere

But euere in oñ
bryght hyt Shon
    Stremeyn clere   10

But Euere me mente
On me hyt blentte
    wyth laughyng' chere   fol. 144r

hyt to be hold'
Was I never' a cold'
    The lonsom lere

Eke stremes ther off
A way Droffe
    Euere the rake

A wykyd wynde
rosse be hende
    At my bake

hyt was so lowde
hyt blew a clowd
    vp ryght   15

hyt was so blake
hyt dyd over lape
    my seght

But Euer I pray
Boyth nygh and day
    Whell I mey speke

The Clowd sso dem
A way to Swym
    In pesyss breke

8. *A cancelled* Hyt *precedes* hyt. *So also in the following line* clu *is crossed out before* cloud.   MS. In my nee.
10. h *and* St *are cancelled before* hyt *and* Stremeyn *respectively.* MS. Scwon.
11. *An extra, uncancelled* But *begins the page and occupies a line by itself.*

That I mey se
The starre so ffre   shynyng' brygh[t]

In the weste
That goyth to reste   Euerry nyght   20

19. may *is written in above the line.*

THE MANUSCRIPTS

UNIVERSITY LIBRARY

Dd.5.76. Described in ULC Cat., I, 285.

1. A quarto, on paper, 52 pages, of 28 lines, hand-writing uniform and of the xvth century but illegible through dirt and friction. . . .

4. A quarto, on paper, 47 pages, double columns, of about 34 lines, badly written, of the xvth century.

Principal contents: Medical notes in a treatise entitled *Liber de diversis rebus et Medicinis ac Unguentis* (page 3).

Numbers 4, 61-66 of the present volume.

Dd. 6.1. ULC Cat., I, 288-89.

A small quarto, on vellum, containing ff. 141, with 21 lines in each page: with rich illuminations and borders. Date, the xvth century.

Principal contents: *Hore Beate Marie Virginis* secundum consuetudinem anglie ecclesie, various devotions, psalms, prayers, etc.

Number 25 of the present volume represents this MS.

Dd.8.2. ULC Cat., I, 334-36.

1. A folio, on parchment, containing ff. 20, with 49 lines in each page. *An Obituary Kalendar* of the brothers, sisters, and benefactors of the Monastery of Kyngton in Wiltshire, by Katerine Moleyns prioress, A.D. 1493, preceded by prayers, a list of the priory lands, the order to receive nuns, &c., and other documents connected with the monastery.

2. Eighteen folio leaves, on vellum, in double columns, with 35 lines in each column, with rich illumined initials and borders, and musical notes. Date, the xvth century.

No. 1C.

Ee. 4.35. ULC Cat., II, 167.

A folio made up of two distinct MSS.

1. On paper, 24 leaves, of about 30 lines, handwriting early xvth century, mutilated in several places: orthography peculiarly corrupt.

2. On parchment, 89 leaves, of about 40 lines, handwriting of the xivth century, very slightly defective at the end: title erased.

Principal contents: various metrical tales; one entitled 'Fabula,' 'The Cheylde and her Stepdame,' 'Robyn Hode,' etc.

Represented here by numbers 16, 20.

Brown, *Reg.*, I, 177, dates the first MS. as early XVI.

Ff.1.6. ULC Cat., II, 286-290.

A quarto, on paper, 159 leaves, of about 30 lines; carelessly written in various hands of the xvth century; imperfect both at the beginning and the end, and in other ways damaged.

Principal contents: a collection of Early English poetry, including several of Chaucer's minor poems, as well as pieces by Occleve and Lydgate.

See also Hammond, *Manual*, 343-6; Greene 340-1; Skeat, *Ox.Ch.*, I, 55; Macaulay's Gower, II, clxvi; Brusendorff, *The Chaucer Tradition*, pp. 187ff: and Robbins, *Sec. Lyr.*, p. xlvi.

Represented here by numbers 40, 41, 42, 43, 44, 46, 68.

Ff.2.38.   ILC Cat., II, 404.

A folio, on paper, 247 leaves, double columns of about 40 lines each, handwriting uniform and of the middle of the xvth century; wants some leaves.

Principal contents: a collection of Early English pieces, chiefly metrical, and chiefly religious; the ten commandments, the deadly sins, a salutation of our lady, etc.

For more complete contents, see Brown, *Reg.*, I, 179-81.

Here represented by numbers 10 and 23.

Ff.5.48.   ULC Cat., II, 505.

A small quarto, on paper, 132 leaves, about 30 lines in each page, damaged in many places, particularly by damp; handwriting generally the same, and of the xvth century.

In the oldest catalogue of the present MSS. all the pieces contained in this volume are attributed to Gilbert Pilkington, but he was in truth no more than a transcriber of one poem.

Principal contents: religious and moral poetry, Myrc's Instructions for Parish Priests, The ABC of Aristotle.

Here represented by numbers 8 and 17.

Gg.4.12.   ULC Cat., III, 152.

Folio, of the xvth century, on vellum, of 204 pages, containing 42 lines, in two columns. The author has not given any name to this work, but speaks of it as "a schort remembrauns of elde stories."

There are marginal annotations in a hand of the xvith century; and in the same hand are verses, English, Latin, and French, on the flyleaves.

Principal contents: John Capgrave's Chronicle from the Creation to A.D. mccccxvii.

Numbers 50, 60.

Gg.4.32.   ULC Cat., III, 177.

A quarto, on parchment, containing ff. 138, with double columns of from 36 to 43 lines. Date, the xivth century. It is written in several different hands.

Principal contents: a miscellaneous collection of theological Documents, Prayers, &c., apparently collected by a cleric for his own use.

No. 11.

Hh.4.12.   ULC Cat., III, 292.

A quarto, chiefly on paper, 99 leaves, about 30 lines in each page, handwriting of the xvth century.

Principal contents: Early English poetry, chiefly by Lydgate; Burgh's *Liber Catonis;* Chaucer's *Parlement of Foules.*

Also described by Hammond, *Manual*, 346-7.

No. 53.

Ii.6.43. ULC Cat., III, 540.

A 12mo, on parchment, ff. 156, with 21 lines in a page. Cent. xv.
Contents: A Manual of Prayers, Hymns, and Meditations in Latin
and English.

No. 1 (A and B).

Mm.4.41. ULC Cat., IV, 294-99.

A folio, on parchment, containing ff. 144, in various hands of the
xivth century. This consists of 4 distinct parts, bound up together.
Contents: chiefly prose works, in Latin, by church fathers:
S. Bernard, Hugo of St. Victor, Bonaventura, Thomas Aquinas, etc.
Part III is devoted to *Tractatus de Jure Romano* chiefly.

Numbers 7, 14, 15.

CORPUS CHRISTI COLLEGE

294. Contains No. 38 on a loose leaf of the xvth century. Brown, *Reg.* I, 211.

405. Contains No. 12. Cent. xiii-xiv. See James, *Cat.C.C.*, II, 277.

GONVILLE AND CAIUS COLLEGE

174/95. James, *G. & C. Cat.* I, 196.
Vellum and paper, several volumes, mostly 8⅝x6¼. Cent. xiv-xvii.
Given by W. Moore.
Part IV, Paper, cent. xv late, very badly written. One quire of
twenty leaves of English poetry.

Numbers 2, 3.

176/97. James, *G. & C. Cat.* I, 201.
Paper, 8½ x 5¾, ff. 114, mostly 31 lines to a page. Cent. xv, rather
roughly written.
Principal contents: Of Phlebotomie, miscellaneous notes, Tract on
Kalendar, scraps of poetry, receipts, Chaucer's *Complaint to His
Purse*, a treatise of medicine.

Only the first 14 lines of Chaucer's *Purse* are in this MS.

No. 47 (which precedes *Purse* on the same page).

EMMANUEL COLLEGE

27. James, pp. 25-27.
Vellum, 9¾x6⅜, ff. 244+1, single and double columns. A number
of tracts were bound together, mostly of cent. xiii. Probably from
Chichester. In a kalendar at the end the dedication to Sompting
Church occurs. Salisbury documents also occur.
Principal contents: miscellanea. Sermons, legends, lessons, inter-
spersed with verses in English, French, and Latin.

Numbers 29-37.

PEMBROKE COLLEGE

307. Described by James, *Pembroke Cat.*, p. 273.
    Vellum, 15⅘x10⅛, ff. 200+2, double columns of 46 lines. Cent. xv,
    early, finely written and ornamented. Probably given by Mr. Mundy.
    Principal contents: Gower's *Confessio Amantis*.
    Numbers 45, 52.

ST. JOHN'S COLLEGE

G.28. James, *St. John's Cat.* p. 230.
    Vellum, 7 x 4¾, ff. 101+8, 24 lines to a page. Cent. xv, well written.
    Donor T.C.S.
    Principal contents: The pore Caitiff. The fly leaves are covered with
    verses of the xvith cent. and one note in English cent. xv.
    No. 51.

TRINITY COLLEGE

B.2.18. James, *Trinity Cat.*, I, 75.
    Paper and vellum, 11¼ x 8½, ff. 114, three parts. Cent. xv and xiv.
    Given by Nevile: belonged to Abp. Matthew Parker.
    Principal contents: Bonaventura *De Vita Christi* in English, etc.
    No. 67.
B.14.39. James, I, 438.
    Vellum, ff. 87 and 93, two volumes bound together. (1) Cent. xiii.
    (2) Cent. xiv, xv.
    Principal contents: English poetry, etc. Poems, hymns, verses, notes,
    in French, Latin, and English.
    See also Brown, *Reg.*, I, 236-37.
    Numbers: 19, 24, 27, 28, 54.
0.1.29. James, III, 33.
    Vellum, ff. 1-119, 43 lines to a page. Cent. xv in a rather current hand.
    Principal contents: religious tracts in English.
    No. 39.
0.2.40. James, III, 142.
    Paper, 8⅜ x 5¾, ff. 163, 31 lines to a normal page. Cent. xv late, in
    a current hand. From Kirkby Bellers.
    Contents: miscellanea, poems, *Secreta Philosophorum*, notes, tracts
    in Latin and English.
    Numbers 21 and 22.
0.2.53. James, III, 169.
    A Note Booke.
    Paper, 8¼ x 5¾, ff. 74, varying number of lines to a page. Cent. xv,
    clearly written.
    Contents: Eng. poetry, miscellaneous notes in prose and verse in
    Eng. and Lat.
    Well represented in the text of this book by numbers 5, 6, 9, 18, 26, 55, 56.
0.9.38. James, III, 495.
    Commonplace book (Glastonbury). Paper, 11⅞ x 4⅜, ff. 90, 51 and

other numbers of lines to a page. Cent. xv, xvi in hands of various degrees of goodness. Originally in a vellum wrapper of which half remains. Tender from damp at each end. Evidently the notebook of a Glastonbury monk.

Principal contents: English didactic poems, many by Lydgate.

Number 59.

R.3.19. James, II, 69.

English Poems by Lydgate, etc. Paper, 10⅝ x 8, ff. 255, mostly 42 lines to a page. Cent. xv late or xvi early, neatly written. Professor Skeat (Chaucer I., p. 56) calls it the "source of most of Stowe's additions to 'Chaucer' " and adds "most of the quires are in a handwriting . . . not far from 1500." Given by Willmer. Belonged to John Stowe.

The complete contents are given by James. See also Skeat, *Ox.Ch.*, I, 56, and especially W.W. Greg, "Chaucer Attributions in MS. R.3.19, in the Library of Trinity College, Cambridge," *MLR*, VIII (1913), 539-40. Five texts are given above: 13, 48, 49, 57, 58.

NOTES TO THE POEMS

1. An Orison to the Trinity

Index 241. This poem occurs also, *Reg,* II, 154, in Bodley 789, fol. 146r; Harley 2406, fol. 8v; Longleat 29, fol. 55v. For notes on Longleat 29, see *Reg.,* II, vi-vii; also Manly and Rickert, I, 343-348.

It is printed from Harley 2406 by Brown, *Rel. Lyr. XV Cent.,* p. 79. Harley and B agree very closely. Harley variants: 6. lighted; 8. one; 20. Lord þou haue mercy on me; 21. And on alle that mercy nede for charite// Amen par amore Amen. In the MS. this poem follows the lovely and moving prayer to the guardian angel, printed *ibid.,* p. 202. C, which Brown groups with them in his notes to the poem, differs considerably from them in the order of the stanzas, in the order of the lines, in some of the lines themselves, and in some of the rimes.

C has been printed by Robbins, *Stud. Phil.,* XXXVI, 472. It is reproduced here for easy comparison.

It is interesting to compare this poem with a shorter *Prayer to the Trinity,* also occurring in Ii. 6. 43 (fol. 120v), printed by Brown, *Rel. Lyr. XV Cent.,* p. 79. Several lines are almost direct parallels. This parallelism may indicate that one poem inspired the other, or, as seems more likely, that the lines are quite conventional. See two articles by Robbins, "Popular Prayers in Middle English Verse," *MP,* XXXVI, 337-350; "Private Prayers in Middle English Verse," *Stud. Phil.,* XXXVI, 467-475.

2. How Sinners Crucify Christ Each Day

This poem, which is not listed by Brown or *Index,* occurs between William Lychefelde's *Complaint of God* and No. 3, the ABC Poem on the Passion, below. James, *Cat.,* I, 196, says that the present poem is also by Lychefelde.

The poem is a sort of dialogue between Christ and man. In the first four stanzas Christ upbraids man for continuing in sin and warns him of the punishments of hell. In the last twelve lines man, realizing how sinful he is, acknowledges the justness of the punishment that will overtake him unless he reforms.

15. *deryst.* Cf. OE *deri(g)an,* 'to harm, hurt, injure, vex.'

3. An ABC Poem on the Passion

This copy is unique. *Index 604.*

The ABC poem of the Middle Ages was a technical exercise in verse-making, the object of which was to compose a song or poem following the letters of the alphabet in their regular order. Four kinds may be distinguished: (1) those in which the first word of each successive stanza begins with the appropriate letter; (2) those in which the first word of each verse begins with the proper letter; (3) those in which each letter is said to signify some event or thing (as in the nursery books: "A is for Archer, B is for Bow," etc.); and (4) those in alliterative lines in which the successive letters indicate the alliterating words, with the result that instead of only one word for each letter we find several.

To the first group belong Chaucer's *ABC;* the two imitations of it printed by MacCracken in *Arch.* CXXXI; the *ABC on the Passion of Christ* printed by Furnivall, *Political, Religious, and Love Poems* (EETS 15), pp. 271-278; a French poem, *The Praise of Women,* and an English translation of it printed together by F. Holthausen in *Arch.* CVIII, 288 ff. One of the second kind is printed by Clark, *The English Register of Godstow Nunnery* (EETS 129), p. 4; by Patterson, *Mid. Eng. Pen. Lyr.,* pp. 137-38; and by Brown, *Rel. Lyr. XV Cent.,* pp. 149-150. The third kind is represented by the present poem; the fourth by the fairly well-known *ABC of Aristotle* (Br 2417, 2645; *Index* 3793, 4155). For other ABC poems see Holthausen, *op. cit.,* and Wells, *Manual,* p. 382 *et passim.*

Most of the ABC poems we know about are devoted to religious subjects: the Blessed Virgin, Christ, the Cross, and the Passion. Some, however, deal with secular matters; e.g., *The Praise of Women* and the *ABC of Aristotle.*

Although we find a certain liveliness about the *ABC of Aristotle* and undoubted sincerity and pathos in the *Invocation to the Cross* (printed by Clark, Patterson, and Brown, as cited above), this kind of poem must be reckoned a *tour de force,* a display of poetic virtuosity, or a mere learner's exercise. MacCracken speaks of "the feeble literary quality" of the two ABC poems printed by him. As in the last two poems in the present volume, the verse-maker always stood in danger of trying harder to follow his pattern than to make a good poem. Skeat, *Ox.Ch.,* I, 59, says of Chaucer's *ABC* that it is "a translation of just that unambitious character which requires no great experience. Indeed, the translation shows one mark of lack of skill; each stanza begins by following the original for a line or two, after which the stanza is completed rather according to the requirements of the rime than with an endeavor to follow the original closely." On the other hand, the poet might become so engrossed in his theme as to forget his pattern. The writer of the present poem, for example, becomes so interested in the idea of the Blessed Virgin as the sole repository of faithfulness to Christ after the disciples fled (cf. Brown, *Rel. Lyr. XV Cent.,* p. 294, note to v. 47) that he departs from his original scheme for almost two entire stanzas.

Some of the versifiers exhibit an amazing ingenuity. Usually, in such poems to the Virgin, the stanza for *X,* owing to the scarcity of words beginning with this letter, begins with *Xps,* or some other common abbreviation for *Christ*. John Marion, however, who wrote the first of the ABC poems printed by MacCracken, cut this Gordian knot by commencing this stanza with "X celente empresse." The same poet, casting about for a word beginning with *K*, finally wrote: "Kalling of Gabriell so ferfull shall be to me." At other times, facing the same problem, the versifier would omit certain letters altogether. Thus Marion concludes with the *X* stanza after omitting *U* and *V*. Our present poet's device is equally transparent. Since it was common in the Middle Ages to follow the letters of the alphabet with the signs for *et* and *con*, some of the pieces, including Chaucer's French source by Deguilleville, even include stanzas beginning with these signs. (See Furnivall, *A One-Text Print of Chaucer's Minor Poems*, Ch. Soc. XXIV, p. 100. Deguilleville's words are "Ethiques" and "Contre.")

The name of "ffyshar," possibly the scribe of the MS., occurs in several places in Part IV of this codex. It appears at the end of a poem in eight-line stanzas, beginning on p. 455 and ending:

which for oure sakys dyd were a croun of thorn
quod fysshar. *Explicit expliciat ludere scriptor eat*

At the bottoms of pages 458 and 459 it is spelled "ffysher" and "ffyssher," respectively. (Cf. James, *Cat. I*, 196 f.)

26. *loth lyden*, 'suffered evil.' Cf. Goth.-*leiþan*, 'to go,' as in *afleiþan*, 'to depart,' OS *līdan* and *far-līdan*, OE *līdan* and *for-līdan* 'to suffer shipwreck,' OHG *līdan*, Mod.HG *leiden;* cf. also Sw. *lida*, 'to suffer, endure, bear (pain, evil, harm, misery)' and Ice. *līda*.

33. *thra*, 'cruel, fierce, eager, keen.' It also occurs in *Rel. Lyr. X V Cent.*, no. 156, v. 30: "fra ded becumin þat is so thra."

4. A Prayer of the Words of Christ on the Cross

Index 7. This copy is unique. Halliwell, *Poems of John Audelay* (Percy Soc., XIV), pp. 62-66, and Whiting, *The Poems of John Audelay* (EETS 184), pp. 58-62, print a poem *De septem verbis Jhesu Christi pendentis in cruce* from Douce 302 (Bodl. 21876). The nineteen 6-line stanzas have the same rime scheme as the present poem. Brown, *Rel. Lyr. X Vth Cent.*, p. 142 ff., prints *The Seven Words from the Cross*, from Arundel 285, fol. 163r. Most of the stanzas begin with *And as þou said. . .* , and the fourth deals with the conversation with the penitent thief. The Douce version agrees with the Camb.Dd. in rime scheme, and the Arundel agrees with it in number of stanzas.

As the *Camb. Univ. Libr. Cat.* notes, this MS. is "imperfect in the beginning and illegible through dirt and friction." I have not attempted to reconstruct any of the lines, but have given only those readings of which I feel reasonably certain. Brown (*Reg.*, I, 166) has given the first two lines as:

And as þy worde cam on þis wyse
To þe thefe w^t þe in paradyse.

Professor Patterson has suggested:

And as þou wolde cryen þis wyse
That þe thefe with the in paradyse
Schulde abide withowten blame.

This last provides a smooth reading of the lines; but though the state of the MS. makes it impossible to say for sure what the first word of v. 2 is, it is fairly evident that it is not *that* nor any of the usual symbols for *þat*.
31. *threst*, 'thirst,' with metathesis. The OE forms are *þurst* and *þyrst*, cognate with OS *thurst*, OHG *durst*, Icel. *þorsti*, and Goth. *þaurstei*.
38. *hende*, Northern ablaut plural.

5. The Psaltere of Ihesu

Unique. *Index* 1730. For a discussion of the type represented by this item and no. 6 see Robbins, *MP*, XXXVI, 337-50, and *Stud. Phil.*, XXXVI, 466-75. In the first of these articles Prayer No. II ends: ".V. thowsand days of pardon."

6. A Prayer in Memory of the Passion

Unique. *Index* 3672. See note to No. 5. These lines follow eight Latin lines on the ills wrought by women.

7. The Wounds of Christ as Remediés Against the Seven Deadly Sins

A. Univ. Libr., Mm.4.41, fol. 137v.
This version is not mentioned by Brown, *Reg*, I, 199, nor in *Index*. It follows, without any break in the MS. and in the same hand, the English paraphrase of *Cur mundus militat*, beginning: "þe saule haskis ryȝt," fol. 137r.

8. A Second Version

B. Univ. Libr., Ff.5.48, fol. 43v (middle) Br. 2660. *Index* 4185 says this poem consists of ten quatrains. Another copy occurs in Jesus Coll. 13, fol. 86v. A different version (Br 2665).is printed in *Rel. Lyr. XIV Cent.* from Harley 2339. The present version differs from that printed by Brown in the order of stanzas and in certain other respects. Stanzas 1, 2, and 5 occur in the same order in both versions; stanzas 3, 4, and 6, 7 of Harley occur here as 6, 7 and 3, 4 respectively. The final stanza differs entirely. The variants from the Harley version are so numerous that for convenient comparison it is here reproduced from Brown (*op. cit.*, pp. 227-28):

Jesus Appeals to Man by the Wounds
MS. Harley 2339

Wiþ scharpe þornes þat weren ful kene,   f. 117b
Myn heed was crowned, ȝe moun wel sene;

The blood ran doun al bi my cheke,
þou proud man, þerfore be meke. 4

Iff þou be wrooþ & wolt take wreche,
Biholde þe lessoun þat I þee teche;
þoruȝ my riȝthond þe nail it gooþ,
þerfore forȝeue & be nouȝt wrooþ. 8

In al my þirst vpon þe rode,
Men ȝauen me drinkis þat weren not gode,
Eysel & galle for to drynke;
Glotoun, þeron I rede þe þenke. 12

Of a clene maiden I was born,
To saue mankynde þat was for-lorn,
To suffre deeþ for mannys synne.
Lecchour, þerfore of lust þou blynne. 16

Thoruȝ my lifthond a nail was dryue—
þenke þou þeron if þou wolt lyue,
And helpe þe pore wiþ almesdede,
If þou in heuene wolt haue þi mede. 20

Wiþ a spere scharp, þat was ful grill,
Myn herte was persid—it was my wil—
For loue of man þat was ful dere;
Enuyous man, of loue þou lere. 24

Arise up, vnlust, out of þi bed,
And biholde my feet, þat are forbled
And nailid faste upon þe tree;
þanke me þerfore, al was for þee. 28

Ihesu, for þi woundis fyue,
þou kepe hem weel in al her lyue
þat þese lessouns ouer wole rede,
And þerwiþ her soulis fede. 32

In *B* the nail goes through the right hand twice, instead of through each hand once, as in the other two (vv. 7, 17). *A* apparently stands somewhere between *B* and Harley, but closer to the former. Although it is conceivable that *A* may be the original poem, it is more probable that in *A*, as in "þe saule haskis ryȝt," the scribe is engaged in paraphrasing a poem already existing. This would account for the supernumerary and hypermetric lines.

A differs from Harley and *B* in order of stanzas and content. Stanzas 1, 3, and 4 occur in Harley as 5, 2, and 3, and in *B* as 5, 2, and 6. Stanza 7 of *A* and Harley is stanza 4 of *B*.

9. Christ Appeals to Man by the Pains of the Passion

Index 2507. Previously printed by James, *Cat.*, III, 173. It is inserted in a blank space in the MS., following part of a long prayer in English, but in a different hand. The prayer ends with the following couplet, written as prose:

Mercy lord of my grete trespace
and euer grammercy of all thy grace.

In its combination of simplicity and force, this poem is reminiscent of the lovely quatrain beginning "Nou goth sonne under wod," *Eng. Lyr. XIIIth Cent.*, p. 1.

10. A Salutacion of Our Lady

Index 1041. Occurs also in MS. Pepys 1584, Art. 8. Audelay's version, printed by Whiting (EETS 184), pp. 155-159, consists of ten 12-line stanzas. It resembles the present poem in many ways: the stanza form, rime scheme, and refrain. A considerable number of the lines are the same, and both poems include many of the same conventional epithets. That the poems are related is obvious, but exactly how is difficult to say without further study of the MSS. For a similar *Salutation* in eleven 12-line stanzas, see Horstmann, *Minor Poems of the Vernon MS.*, pp. 134-137.

Salutations, which go back eventually to the Annunciation (Luke i: 29 ff.), were fairly numerous in the ME period. Brown's *Register* lists eight, one of which occurs in five MSS.

9. *ryse*, 'twig, branch.'

75. *postlys*, 'apostles.'

82. *maynpernoure*. See *OED, s.v.* MAINPERNOR. This is a legal term meaning a surety for a prisoner's appearance in court on a certain day. In Audelay's version (Whiting, v. 118) this line reads: "Mare, þou be *our* mayne p*aroure*." The glossary explains *Mayne* as "adj. main," and *paroure* as "sb. jewel." The *Ff* reading seems the better of the two.

11. Ave Maria

Unique. *Index* 1064. It occurs between an expanded *Pater Noster* and the twelve articles of the Creed. See also No. 30 below.

12. Heyle, God ye schilde

Unique. Both Brown (Br 655) and James (*Cat.* II, 277) seem confused in their accounts of this piece. The former calls it "A salutation of the B.V.—nine long lines with medial rime"; the latter (p. 279, item 10) says "In a charter hand: Verses . . . 22." He then prints the first nine lines occurring on page 22, skips the next seven, then prints the last of the long lines, writing "8 lines" after them in parentheses. *Index* 1047 and Wells, *Manual* (Sixth Suppl., pp. 1467 and 1521) repeat Brown. I here reproduce the entire page to clarify the matter.

What we have here is not a single long poem at all, but several short pieces, as is indicated by the marginal scribal lines and the scribal note opposite v. 10. The first two of these translate or paraphrase Latin originals, a common practice in the M.E. period. See Brown, *Eng. Lyr. XIIIth Cent.*, pp. 191, 192 (note to No. 30) and pp. 193, 194 (note to No. 33).

The *Salutation* thus consists of at most only *six* long lines, and possibly of only two.

The last three lines are gnomic and should, perhaps, have been printed
with the "Wise Sayings," numbers 56-61 below.

Corpus Christi 405, p. 22

Quem fortuna leuis miserum facit esse beatum
Sic fortunatum degradat hora breuis
Of noman liche makeʒ hap in a stound many Riche
Hym can be so fette Weryt fyrst Hym fond sone sette
Est res exsempli confusa superbia Templi   5
Ilk wisman takeʒ forbysne wat pride maket
Of wylum templeis wyh helde non cyre til hem pres
Heyle god ye schilde/modyr Holy kyng bere milde
Hefne yat in kepyng haʒ an world vit outyn hondyng
Chaungon hys ryhte Oon kynde sosone michte   10
Yat dede nere synne schuld chyld conseyue vyt ynne
Als sune schene/smyt your glas wer nis ysenne
Wyt outyn tene Wemles bar Child maydyn clene
Al vnder sunne catel is Wyt swynk her yvonne
Ay kept wyt drede so fulnap yat ye ne schode   15
And left vit sourwe van deʒ comyt after amorwe

3. MS. astound.
These English lines are immediately succeeded by the following Latin
notes, here reproduced from James, *Cat.*, II, 279-280.

i. Alban super aquam

i nauis	curranth. alban ar. lyn	
i plenus	De famylia alban. intro	unde versus Ibern.
Lactu	De myntyr alban. Jn.	

Curranth. ar alban lyn alban muntyr de laan.

	Lagemia continet	xxxiᵃ	
	Conactia cont.	xxxᵃ	
Quinque partes	Mydgya cont.	xviiᵃ	cantres
Hibernie	Ultonya cont.	xxxvᵃ	
	Memonya cont.	lxxᵃ	

Qualibet Candreda continet .xxx. villatas et quelibet villata
potest sustinere cccᵗᵃˢ vaccas in pasturis et vacce sit diuid-
antur in quatuor armenta. Nullam illarum appropinquabit
ad aliam. Item quolibet (?) villa habet octo carucat terre.

The metrics of the long English lines are quite interesting; the parts
of each line are bound together with medial rime, and the latter half of
the line is usually much longer than the first. This is somewhat similar
to the practice in the *Tale of Gamelyn*.

13. To His Mistress

Unique. Brown 1137 calls it *An Orison to the Blessed Virgin. Index*
1838 describes it more accurately as *An Epistle to his Mistress*, since only
the opening stanza is addressed to the B.V. It should probably have been
included among Love Songs and Complaints.

3. double superlative.
16. *intemerate*, 'inviolate, chaste, pure.'
62. *deueure*, 'devoir, duty.'
64. These are conventional mediaeval comparisons. They occur in the

Latin poem which follows (No. 14) and, of course, in the English translation, vv. 13-20.

14. Cur Mundus Militat

Brown lists ten MSS. of the English version (Br 2649), of which three have been printed (the first two of these are there noted): (1) Harley 1706, fol. 93r and again at 150r (Horstmann, *Richard Rolle*, ii, 374-75); (2) Lambeth 853, p. 32 (Furnivall, *Hymns to the Virgin and Christ*, pp. 86-87; Wülcker, *Æ Lesebuch*, ii, 14-15); (3) Trin. Coll. 181, foll. 169v-170r (Brown, *Rel. Lyr. XIV Cent.*, pp. 237-39.)

In his notes to the poem (p. 287) Brown lists the following Latin editions: (1) Wright, *Poems of W. Mapes* (Camd. Soc.), p. 147; (2) Daniel, *Thes. Hymn.*, ii, 379; (3) Dreves, *Anal.*, xxxiii, 267; (4) Migne, *Patrol. Lat.*, clxxxiv, col. 1313.

The present version is mentioned by Brown, *Reg.*, I, 199; and listed separately in *Index*, item 3475.

For notes on the MSS. of the Latin versions see *Univ. Libr. Camb. Cat.* description of Ee.6.6 (item 5) and Mm. 4.41 (item 9). See also Wright, *op. cit.*

The present English and Latin versions are exactly parallel, except that the English version adds one stanza (see below). The Latin version parallels those in Wright, Migne, Daniel, and Dreves, excepting that stanzas 8 and 9 are transposed.

According to Brown's note (*Rel. Lyr. XIV Cent.*, p. 287) "Migne's text differs from the others in arrangement, the last four stanzas, according to the usual order, being transferred to the beginning." A careful examination shows that Migne's text follows the usual order: it differs in that it begins with four stanzas not occurring in the other versions.

The text printed by Dreves (Cod. Luciliburgen.84. "Bearbeitung oder vorlage des bekannten *Cur Mundus militat*"), although it follows the usual order, differs in two respects: (1) It is written in 3-line stanzas, *aaa*, etc.; (2) stanza 9 has been omitted, and stanza 10 expanded into two stanzas, so that the content of stanza 10 (according to the usual order) makes up stanzas 9 and 10 in the Dreves text.

The text printed by Daniel omits stanza 3; otherwise it parallels that printed by Wright.

Excepting Dreves's, which is in three-line stanzas, *aaa*, all the Latin versions, including the one here reproduced, are in four-line stanzas, *aaaa*.

15. Translation of *Cur Mundus Militat*

The English versions (beginning "Whi is þis world biloued," etc.), printed by Furnivall, Horstmann, and Brown are parallel, except that Horstmann's omits lines 35 and 36. In these three versions stanza 10 of the Latin occurs as stanza 7. Stanza 8 of the other four Latin versions occurs as stanza 9 in the present MS. and in the printed English texts. Whereas the other texts are written in couplets, the present text follows the rime scheme of the original, *aaaa*, with the addition of somewhat clumsy and irregular internal rime. In the verses which he has added the *Mm* translator suggests that he has been at some pains to follow his original closely, although at times his rendering of the Latin is rather free. Although an examination of all the English and Latin MSS. would be necessary to determine their relationship with finality, it seems probable that the printed Eng. versions are based upon the text represented in Mm.4.41 rather than upon that represented by the other Latin texts.

The theme, as the number of MSS. of this and similar poems indicates, the transitoriness of human life and glory contrasted with the eternal life of the hereafter, was extremely popular throughout the Middle Ages. For a discussion of this theme and for the text of a similar poem (BM Adds. 37049, fol. 31), see Part IV, "Mahnung des Todes," pp. 26ff. of an article by Karl Brunner "Mittelenglische Todesgedichte," *Arch.* 167; 20-35. I note a few lines that are either identical or very similar:

Mm	*Adds.*
13–20	22–30
25	31
26, 27	31–33
35	52

There is also an extended discussion of the *ubi sunt* motive in Hammond, *Eng. Verse*, pp. 169-171.

24. dusyper, *cf. NED, s.v. DOUZEPERS, the twelve peers.*

41. bryne, *brows,* hence *'eyes.' Cf. OE, gen. pl., brūna; Icl. brȳnn; Sw. ŏgonbryn, 'eyebrows.'*

44. *I.e.,* St. Austin's.

16-19. Warnings of Death

No. 16. Ee.4.35, fol. 24r, "Whan thy hed quakes *memento."* Dated "early xv cent." by *Univ. Cat.,* but assigned to the early XVI cent. by Brown (*Reg.,* I, 178).

No. 17. Ff.5.48, fol. 43v, "When þi hed whaketh/*memento."* Dated XV cent. by *Univ. Cat.;* no date is given by Brown.

No. 18. Trin. O.2.53, fol. 72r, "Whan thyn heed shaketh *memento."* Assigned to the XV cent. by James (*Cat.,* III, 169); to the XV-XVI cent. by Brown (*Reg.,* I, 253).

Brown describes the *Signs of Death* (Br 2583) as a poem of "eight lines (in some MSS. twelve lines)." The eleven MSS. he lists as follows: (1) Bodl. 1045, fol. 183v; (2) Bodl. 2305, fol. 91r; (3) Bodl. 10234, fol. 35v; (4) Bodl. 12514, fol. 148v; (5) Univ. Lib. Camb. Ee.4.35, Part I, fol. 24r; (6) Univ. Lib. Camb. Ff.5.48, fol. 43v; (7) Queen's Camb. 13, fol. 64r; (8) Trin. Camb. 1157, fol. 72r; (9) Royal 8.CXII, fol. 1v; (10) ? Eton Coll. 34; (11) Vatican MS, Ottoboni 626.

Index 4035 lists 14 MSS., in the first seven of which the lines appear as a tag in the *Fasciculus Morum;* in the latter seven it occurs separately. Robbins notes that one version, Brown's (7), is printed in James's *Catalogue.*

Brown, *Eng. Lyr. XIII Cent.*, prints (p. 130) a twenty-two-line version, *"Proprietates Mortis,"* Trin. Coll. 43, fol. 73v, beginning: "Wanne mine eyhnen misten." In his notes (pp. 220-22) he discusses the sources of these lists of signs and prints several other versions of the longer (twelve-twenty-two lines) forms of the poem.

The longer and the shorter forms are catalogued separately by Brown, *Reg.*, II: Br 2562, twenty-two lines; Br 2575, fourteen lines; Br 2584, eighteen lines; Br 2581, four lines; Br 2583, eight lines; Br 2582, eight long lines. So also *Index.* The three versions reproduced in this volume are all of eight lines.

No. 19 of this volume (*Index* 4046) is the only four-line version. The manuscript is of the thirteenth century.

20. The vij vertwys Agyn the vij dedley Synys

Index 469. The poem also occurs in Harley 1706, fol. 206r.

21. Augustinus de peccatis venialibus

Unique, *Index* 806. The poem is preceded in the MS. by four completed and two unfilled horoscopes.

2, 32. *Than myster wore,* 'than is fitting and proper' (OED).

22. Decem remedia contra peccata venialia üt patebit inferus

A unique copy. *Index* 3866.

2. *for doys,* 'fordoes.'

23. The Five Goostly Wyttys

Index 1126. Occurs also in Pepys 1584 (art. 13), Harley 1706, fol. 207v; Harley 2339, fol. 121v.

This poem is embedded in a collection of similar pieces. Three of them, "The Seven Werkis of merci bodili," "The Seven Werkis of merci gostli," and "The Five bodyly Wyttys," have been printed from Lambeth 491, fol. 295v, by Bülbring, *Arch.*, LXXXVI, 388-89. "The Seven Deedly Synnes" has been printed from Harley 1706, fol. 205v, by Heuser (*Bonn. Beit.*, XIV, 205). The title ("The Seuen vertues contrarie to the seven deadly synnes") has been mistakenly inserted before the poem beginning at fol. 33r. This is really a poem on the wounds of Christ and the sins they remedy; see numbers 7 and 8 above. It has been printed from Harley 2339 (foll. 117v-118r) by Brown, *Rel. Lyr. XIV Cent.*, pp. 227, 28.

24. Lines on the Old Testament Worthies

Unique. *Index* 109.

Such brief translations as these are rather common in ME MSS. See note to No. 12 above.

1. looset 'locked.' Cf. Sw. låsa.

25. A Riming Exhortation

Index 317. This poem was added (Brown, *Reg.*, I, 66) by a later hand to a Latin text of the Hours of the B.V. (Br 206). The poem also occurs in Ashmole 59 (fol. 73r; vv. 1-9 missing). Similar series of precepts in *-ly* are found in Br 211, 510, 1985, and 1999. The present poem differs from the others in using *-ly* lines only at the beginning (vv. 1-3) and in the middle (vv. 10-13).

Vv. 16-19, which are proverbial, occur as the final couplet of a group of proverbs in No. 62 below.

Br 1999 is printed by James, *Cat.* (St. John's 71, fol. 104r):

> Siȝe and sorwe depeli:
> moorne and wepe enwardli.
> Praie and þenke deuoutli:
> loue & longe continuelli.

26. Admonition Against Swearing

Unique. *Index* 1255. This item, not listed by Brown, occurs between a Latin poem, "*Ad loca stellata duc nos katerina beata*" and another beginning: "*Veni creator spiritus.*"

27. Health of Body and Soul

Unique. *Index* 1924. According to Skeat (cf. James, *Cat.*, I, 438) the scribe of this MS. was a Norman. No. 27 is followed by a poem to the Virgin, beginning: "Leudie ic þenke þe wid herte suiþe milde" (Brown, *Eng. Lyr. XIII Cent.*, p. 42).

28. Penaunce is in Herte Reusing

Unique. *Index* 2746. The MS. is thirteenth cent.

1. *reusinge*, 'rueing, feeling sorry.'
3. *edbote*, 'restitution, amends.'   7. *ageet*, 'passes away.'

29-37. Parts of the Mass in English Rime

This collection from the late thirteenth century is a good example of private prayers for the use of literate laymen. See the Notes to No. 1 above for pertinent articles by R. H. Robbins. See also *Sec. Lyr. XIV and XV Cent.*, xxii *passim*.

No. 29. *Index* 2704. Like the *Pavia* version printed by Thomson in MLN xlix, p. 236, a rimed elaboration of the paternoster. The present poem is far superior to the *Pavia*, whose text differs so considerably from it that they have scarcely anything in common except their ultimate source.

No. 30. *Index* 1062. 'A variant text.' Wells *Manual* (First Suppl., p. 991) says that unprinted texts of this poem are to be found in St. John's Coll. Camb. S. 30 (p. 269; early XIV) and in Lambeth 559 (fol. 15v; ?XIV).

No. 31. *Index* 2769.

No. 32. Unique. *Index* 3884. Printed by Robbins, MP XL, p. 140; and by McGarry, *The Eucharist in Middle English Verse*, p. 224.

No. 33. Unique. *Index* 1599.

No. 34. Unique. *Index* 177.

No. 35. *Index* 580. For other versions see 1571, 1600, 1952.

No. 36. Unique. *Index* 2187.

No. 37. Unique. *Index* 3100.

38. On the "Leaps" Which Christ Took

Unique copy. *Index* 268. Mentioned by James (*Cat.*, II, 70-71): "*Varia opuscula Hugonis de Sancto Victore. . . cent. XIII.*"

This somewhat amusing poem calculates how far Christ "leaped" when he ascended into heaven. The poem is followed in the MS. by some notes in Latin and French on the distance from the earth to the moon, from the moon to the sun, from the sun to the stars, etc.

A similar poem based on a mathematical computation of the number of drops of blood Christ shed is printed in *Rel. Lyr. XV Cent.*, p. 133.. The note to the poem (pp. 322, 23) explains how the number of wounds was computed as 5,475 and the number of drops of blood as 547,000.

An even more similar poem, *Spacium de terra ad celum*, *Index* 2794, employing the same figures, is printed by Hahn, *Archiv* cvi, p. 350. It consists of twenty-seven short lines in couplets. The present poem, which seems from internal evidence to be derived from it or from its source, elaborates further by introducing the idea of Christ's ascension. Although the piece occurs in the MS. as twenty long lines in couplets, the presence and the regularity of the internal rime suggest it may have been intended as forty short lines riming *abab*.

These are not the same "leaps" as those named in Cynewulf's *Christ*, vv. 715-750, a mystical interpretation of *Cant.* 2:8. See Cook, *The Christ of Cynewulf* (Albion Series), Boston, 1910, pp. 143-44.

39. On the Value of Prayer and Meditation

Unique copy. *Index* 826. The poem starts at the end of a prose treatise in English on prayer, *Pupilla Oculi.*

40. Alas, Alas, and Alas Why

Index, 139. Printed, with Nos. 42 and 44, by Robbins, *Sec. Lyr. XIV and XV Cent.*, pp. 156, 155, 158.

The MS. (Ff.1.6) in which this poem occurs contains some Chaucer material and is closely related to Bodl. Tanner 346. See Brusendorff, *The Chaucer Tradition*, pp. 187 ff. The *Alas* poem follows "Now wold I fayne sum myrthis make," printed in *Rel. Ant.*, I, 25. The latter is signed "A god when," which the ULC Cat. (II, 289) takes to be the name of the author of some of these poems; but Hammond (*Manual*, pp. 343-44) disagrees. "Several scribes," she says, "have signed their names, Lewestoun, Calverley, Nicholas 'plenus amoris,' and the man who uses the rebus of a tun, below which is a scroll with two pendent fishes, and the motto

'A God when.' This is perhaps the rebus of Lewestoun (luce-tun), although the hand does not seem the same as that of Chaucer's Purse, which is signed Lewestoun. But the remark in *Reliq. Antiq.* I: 27 as to the English poet 'Godwhen' is of no meaning."

The Chaucer items are *PF, Anel., Purse,* and "Thisbe" from *LGW. Ff* also contains the *Venus;* but not the *Mars,* which in most MSS. precedes as a companion piece. It also has *The Cuckoo and the Nightingale,* once printed, although not from this MS., among the works of Chaucer.

41. Alas What Planet Was I Born Vndir

Index, 159. See note above to No. 40, which immediately precedes in the MS. In the space between the end of No. 41 and the beginning of the one that follows it is written "Crocit Dycon" (or Dyton).

13. *apeire,* 'to grow or become less, deteriorate, decay.'

42. The Lover Wishes His Lady Recovery

Unique. *Index* 383. These two stanzas, which follow Clanvowe's *The Cuckoo and the Nightingale,* are not noted by Hammond or the ULC Cat. There is no signature, and the lower half of the leaf is blank. Brusendorff (p. 187, n. 2) says that this part (foll. 22-28) is a special inset in the MS.

43. Lament

Unique. *Index* 1331. See notes to No. 40 above. Described in *Index* as "five stanzas rime-royal and Envoy," but printed correctly as three stanzas in *Sec. Lyr., loc. cit.* Hammond (*Manual,* p. 344) says that this piece occupies fol. 20r and 20v and that it consists of "five stanzas of seven lines and four lines of another." Two facts indicate that this is not the case. First, these three stanzas on fol. 20r all bear the same refrain, whereas those on fol. 20v have none. Secondly, at the top of fol. 20v the caption ("Margery Hungerford w^{t}owte variaunce") indicates the beginning of a new poem (No. 44 below).

44. Without Variance

Index 4059.
See note to No. 43 above.

45. A Troubled Lover's Apostrophe to Death

Unique copy. *Index* 2412. At the top of the page occurs the name Mundy. The piece is written again at the bottom of the page, but so faintly as to be almost indecipherable.

46 A Compleint vn to Dame Fortune Capitulo xxviii

Unique copy. *Index* 2568. The ULC Cat. says (II, 289-90): "This piece appears to be an extract from cap. xxvii and xxviii of some larger poem. In the former chapter the burden of each stanza is: "Of alle oure synnys god make a delyueraunce. . . .""

That the piece dealt with contemporary conditions is indicated both by the poem itself and by the fact that in the MS. it directly follows "How myschaunce regnyth in Ingleland" (Wright, *Political Poems*, II, 238).

22. See Lydgate's *Measure is Treasure* (Br 1348; MacCracken, II, 776; unique in Harley 2255), v. 72.

47. A Pure Balade of Love

Unique. *Index* 1827. On the lower half of the page are the first two stanzas of Chaucer's *Purse*, printed by MacCracken, *MLN*, XXVII, 228-29. MacCracken assigns the MS. to the middle of the XV century.

48. The Dyscryuyng of a Fayre Lady

Index 1300. First printed by Stowe, 1561, under the title of *A Balade Pleasaunt*. This poem and the one that follows belong to the class of satires on women, a rather common theme in the fifteenth century and earlier. It abounds in that type of irony which says the opposite of what it means, using the oblique approach. The title in *Trin.* is similar to that of Lydgate's *A Satirical Description of His Lady*. That the *Dyscryuyng* is an imitation of Lydgate's longer satire would appear both from the mode of expression and the spirit. See Halliwell, *Lydgate's Minor Poems* (Percy Soc.), II, 199, and Skeat, *Ox.Ch.*, VII, xiii. See also No. 208 in *Sec. Lyr. XIV and XV Cent.*

No. 48 is here reproduced for two reasons besides the fact that it is lots of fun, Skeat to the contrary notwithstanding. First, someone in the fifteenth century evidently considered it of significance, since it occurs in the important MS., Trin. R.3.19. Secondly, it will clear up a point raised by Skeat (*Ox.Ch.*, I, 42). According to him the piece is "very unpleasant and scurrilous, and alludes to the wedding of 'queene Iane' as a circumstance that happened many years ago." But in another place (VII, xiii) he writes: "The author says that when he was fifteen years old, he saw the wedding of Queen Jane; and that was so long ago that there cannot be many such alive. As Joan of Navarre was married to Henry IV in 1403, he was born in 1388, and would have been sixty-two in 1450." Skeat apparently misread the poem. Vv. 36-43 (st. 6) do not refer to the age of the author but to that of the subject of the work. It will also correct the impression given by *Index* 1300 that the main subject of the poem is "the marriage of Joan of Navarre to Henry IV in 1403." Thus to connect her with an event long past is simply an oblique way (still in everyday use by radio funny men and others) of saying that the lady in question is well past the first bloom of youth.

A comparison of the *Trin.* text and that of Stowe will show how much the latter "modernized" the spelling after fewer than a hundred years. No. 48 has not been printed since Chalmers (Hammond, *Manual*, p. 428).

49. O Mosy Quince

Index 2524. Printed by Stowe and by his successors until Chalmers;

see Hammond, *Manual*, p. 442. All these editors omit the second stanza.

Skeat (*Ox.Ch.*, VII, 297) prints two stanzas from Stowe, very similar to the stanza omitted in the prints and obviously going back to the same source. MacCracken, EETS 192, p. 708, prints two versions of the omitted stanza from Camb. Trin. R.3.20, and a third from Bod. Fairfax (No. 45 of his Lydgate Canon).

10. *enbonyd*, corrected by Stowe to *enbolned*, pp. of *embolen, enbolnen*, 'swollen', etc.

20. *bawsyn*, 'fat, unwieldy, swollen.' *NED s.v.* Bausond. See also Wright, *The English Dialect Dictionary*.

21. *Saint Barbara*. Earlier, the patron saint in time of danger from thunderstorms and fire; at this time the protector of artillerymen and miners.

gonne. Possibly a play on *gun/gown* is intended here.

24. *barkfate*, 'tanner's vat.'

50. When Women Will Reform

Unique. *Index* 3946. Occurs on last flyleaf of Gg.4.12, with other verses and scraps: "High Towres" (no. 63 below) and several lines from Chaucer (*Troil.*, I, 400 ff.), beginning: "If loue be not, Lord what fele I so." The rhetorical device of leading up to and emphasizing an idea by indirection was a favorite during the ME period. See "When to Trust a Woman— Never" (Dyboski, *Songs, Carols, and other Misc. Poems*, EETSES, CI, pp. 114-15 and Robbins, *Sec. Lyr.*, p. 103). It begins: "Whan netillis *in* wynter bere rosis rede/& thornys bere figg*is* naturally/& bromes bere appyll*is in* eue*ry* mede. . . ." and carries the refrain: "Than put i*n* a woma*n* yo*ur* trust & confidens." See also Wright's *Songs and Carols*, no. LVIII. No. 95 in Dyboski, which follows a similar vein, bears the refrain:

> Of all creatures women be best
> *Cuius contrariu*m *verum est.*

51. Against the Friars and the Fryers Complaynt

Unique copy. *Index* 3697, 161. Cf. James, *Cat.*, p. 230.

Brown calls this piece "Verses against the friars—nine 6-line stanzas." Wells, *Manual*, p. 957, repeats Brown. Francis L. Utley, *Harv. Theol. Rev.*, xxxviii, suggests that they are separate poems. That the scribe regarded them as a single poem might be inferred from the absence of any break in the MS. The title to the latter part has been supplied in the margin by a later hand. The scribe has drawn braces to show the rime schemes, and has put a ¶ opposite the first word of the first quatrain. *Index* lists them separately, describing the first part (3697) as *Verses against the Friars*, and the second (161) as *An Ironic Lament of the Friars in answer to 3697*. In any event, since each of the parts has more meaning in juxtaposition with the other than by itself, it is probably just as safe to look upon it as a sort of dialogue, a plaint and response reminiscent of Chaucer's *Fortune*. See also No. 2, above. But however one chooses to regard them, the verses are equally enjoyable. See *Jack Upland* and Skeat's notes (VII, 492 ff.).

Stanza division is indicated in the MS. by marginal lines.

4. *aposen,* 'confront with objections and hard questions' (OED).

24. *werynge clopes,* similar to many expressions still to be heard in the South; e.g., "drinking liquor, readin' books, walkin' shoes," etc.

52. Punctuation Poem

Unique (Br 2450), *Index* 3809. James, *Cat.,* pp. 274-5, says: "On [fol.] 197b are English verses:

> Trusty seldom to their ffrendys uniust, etc.
> Then copied again with different punctuation."

Previously printed by Kreuzer, *RES,* XIV, 323; and by Robbins, *Sec. Lyr. XIV and XV Cent.,* p. 101, with two other punctuation poems. The latter prints the stanza once, punctuating it with periods as in the second copy in the MS. Kreuzer's editing would mislead students of punctuation. He remarks: "In this case the scribe has copied the text twice in order to bring out the double interpretation." This is literally true, but not in the way in which Kreuzer's presentation would lead one to believe. Using no mark of punctuation except the period, he presents an *A* version, complimentary to the friars, and a *B* version derogatory, by shifting the periods. As a matter of fact, however, both versions are punctuated exactly alike in the MS., so far as periods are concerned. The double interpretation is indicated in the MS., not by a shifting of the periods, but by virgules drawn after all the lines except v. 3 in the *A* version. This device changes the lines from run-on to end-stop and thus makes clear the poet's intention. Further, the scribe has drawn a brace after the lines in this version and after it has written "TrV" (= True?).

53. Alas! quid eligam ignoro

Index 655. Occurs also in BM Addit. 29729, fol. 3r (17 stanzas). In the MS. it comes between "A Lament" (fol. 89r), in which every stanza ends: "All women may be ware by me" and Chaucer's *PF.*

5. *layfee,* 'the laity, lay people collectively.'

37. *ciuilistre,* an expert in Roman civil law.

45. *officiall,* the presiding officer or judge, in the Church of England, of an archbishop's, bishop's, or archdeacon's court.

> *Advocate,* one who is authorized or appointed to plead in court.
> *Proctour,* agent for collection of tithes and other church dues.
> *Notary,* clerk, one authorized to draw up documents.

65. *bewavyd,* 'bewaved, blown about.'

> *procellows,* 'stormy.'

74. *Possessioner,* an endowed clergyman or ecclesiastic.

> *Mendinant, mendiuant* 'beggar' in OF; see Bradley-Stratmann.

100. *Vngiltles,* double negative.

125. *parell,* verb, 'to clothe, dress, attire, array.' *parell with,* 'to dress as fashionably or richly.'

130. *Vggyd,* 'to inspire or affect with dread, loathing, or disgust.'

149. Chaucerian allusion.
166. *poo*, 'peacock.'
167. *refreyt*, a refrain or burden.

54. The Poor Widow and the Rich Man

Index 106. Brown dates the MS. as XIII century, but does not mention this item.

2. *hurede*, 'hired, bribed.'
6. *firbernen = forbrennen*.
8. *honde of honde*, 'at close quarters, side by side.'
9. *parlesie*, 'palsy.'
10. *firbraid*, OE *forbregdan*, *-brēdan*, 'pervert, corrupt.'
The meaning of these lines is not entirely clear. Perhaps they represent an amateur poet's attempt to versify a familiar story.

55. Exhortation to Study

Unique. *Index* 726. A Latin poem, entitled *Deferencia* and beginning: *Silua tenet leporem sapientia lingua leporem*, follows in a different hand.

56. The Vanity of Worldly Lusts

Unique. *Index* 3905. Cf. Chaucer's *Stedefastnesse*.

57. The Transitoriness of Worldly Prosperity

Unique. *Index* 3493. See description of MSS. Occurs at top of fol. 67r; the lower half is blank, as is all of fol. 66. James (*Cat.*, II, 71) calls it "Two 7-line stanzas marked *vacat* as being a fragment." Although the lines have a familiar ring to a reader of fifteenth-century verse, I have been unable to identify the poem of which James says this is a fragment. The theme is, of course, encountered throughout the ME period.

58. Of the iiij Complexions

Index 2624. Printed from Harley 2251 by Robbins, *Sec. Lyr.*, p. 72.
This poem (Br 1617) occurs also in Ashmole 59 (3 stanzas; fol. 71v) and Harley 2251 (fol. 79r). A 12-line variant of the Latin sections occurs in Balliol 354, No. 110. Published by Dyboski, *Songs, Carols, and Miscellaneous Poems*, EETSES 101, pp. 139-40.
It seems possible that in the present poem we may have an earlier version of the three-stanza *The Disposicion of the iiij Complexyons*, printed by MacCracken, *Minor Poems of John Lydgate*, II, 731-32, from Trinity R.3.21 (fol. 289r) and II, 737, from Harley 2255, as a part of *A Pageant of Knowledge*, beginning "Thys worlde is born up by astates seuyn." Various parts of this "pageant" have been published as separate poems: e.g., *Seven Wise Counsels* (with collation of 5 MSS. by Förster, *Arch.*, CIV, 297); *On the Mutability of Human Affairs* (Halliwell, *MP*, pp. 193-98). This last is printed from Harley 2255, not 2251, as MacCracken says (I, xxiii).

I am unable to identify the author of the Latin lines translated in this poem, although I am satisfied that their source is the *Secreta Secretorum*, which was immensely popular for several centuries (Cf. Steele, *Secrees of Old Philisoffres*, EETSES LXVI, pp. xiv-xv). Steele states that he has personally examined thirty Latin versions in the BM alone. He refers to a very early Spanish, four Italian, and five French independent versions and adds: "I believe there were also some early German translations." The title of the preceding poem in the MS. suggests that we may have here a translation of his source made by Lydgate before reworking it to fit the pattern of his longer poem on the theme of man's difficulty in being "stedfast of lyuyng." The former poem is headed (James, *Cat.*, II, 71) "A tretis of the iiij seasons of the yere that is to say *ver, estas authumnus,* and *yemps* [copieyed by Ihon Lydgate as aperyth in his book of yᵉ secretes to Alysaunder from Aristotyll]."

MacCracken does not mention the present MS. in either volume of his Lydgate. Explaining why he has called the piece a pageant, MacCracken speaks of its being presented "as a school play, like its original in Ausonius." (I, xxiii) Unfortunately, he fails to identify this Ausonius or to specify the work which is the "original"; and an examination of the collected works of Decimus Magnus Ausonius (*c.* 310-393) fails to reveal any similar piece which might clarify the ascription, unless it be *Ludus Septem Sapientum* (Loeb ed., pp. 310 ff.). This poem is described by Sister Marie Jose Byrne (*Prolegomena to an Edition of the Works of Decimus Magnus Ausonius*, pp. 58-59) as follows: "The LSS was composed in 390 and dedicated to Pacatus, who was proconsul of Africa in that year. . . It contains a prologue and a speech by the Ludius, who names the seven wise men and the saying attributed to each, after which the sages themselves appear one after another and explain their proverbs. These are given first in Greek, then in Latin." There is nothing in Ausonius' poem which even suggests Lydgate's pageant.

However, on pp. 406 ff. in Peiper's edition of the works of Ausonius, a similar poem entitled *Septem Sapientum Sententiae* is printed in Chapter XXII, which is devoted to works formerly attributed to Ausonius and which bears the heading *INCERTORUM: Olim cum Ausonianis edita.* This poem differs from the genuine, as Byrne notes, in length and verse form. In it each of the sages explains his saying in a poem of seven lines. It is possible that MacCracken has somehow confused the *Seven Wise Counsels* printed by Förster with the title of this pseudo-Ausonian poem. The former, headed "Doctrynes of Wisdame" in one MS., consists of seven stanzas, each of which is devoted to one of the worldly virtues: Prudence, Justice, Temperance, Discretion, etc.

The exact source of the "Pageant" as a whole is thus a matter of some uncertainty. Förster, *op. cit.*, even expresses some doubt that the portion printed by him actually comes from a Latin original.

In *The Gouernaunce of Prynces*, translated by James Yonge (1422), EETSES LXXIV, we find a prose version of the present poem. Steele, in his prefatory note, states that the greater portion of this text (the third version) is a direct translation of the French version made by Jofroi of Waterford. That the substance of our poem occurs twice is indicated by the following chapter heads:

> That the scyence of Physnomy, and of the iiij maneres of complexcions, and of al colours and lymmes of manys body, the tokenys of what condycionys they sholde bene, aftyr the same science, Capitulum Lviij^m.
>
> Of that same science of Physnomye, in a shortyr manere . . . . Capitulum Lix^m.

In a third chapter also the same ideas are presented:

> Of the gouernaunce of helth of manys body aftyr Physike. Cap. Lxj^m.

See also the body of chapters 58 (Steele, ed., pp. 219-220) and 61 (pp. 236-237). Substantially the same discussion of the four complexions is to be found in Gower (*CA*, VII, 11393), whose source, according to Steele, is the *Secreta*.

Thus, it seems fairly clear that this part of the "Pageant," at least, has its origin in the *Secreta Secretorum*, of which Lydgate made a poetical version (L132 in MacCracken's Lydgate Canon), rather than in Ausonius.

12. Reference to the Latin (*cantans*) shows *chauntere* to be a better reading than the Harley MS. *champioun* on both lexical and prosodic grounds.

59. Proverbs in Rimed Couplets

Index 3170. James (*Cat.*, III, 495) says that this MS. is "evidently the note-book of a Glastonbury monk."

Brown does not mention this collection of proverbs among his first lines (*Reg.*, II). In the MS. this item is preceded by *An Admonition against Swearing by the Mass*, fol. 69v (printed by Dyboski from Balliol 354 and by Greene from the Trinity MS.), and by a *Quid Inde* poem of seven lines (*Rel. Ant.*, I, 57). It is followed, 70v-77v, by *De S. Hilda*. James *Cat.* III, p. 501.

14. *travell*, 'travail'; *parell*, 'peril.'

20. *bate*, 'contention, strife, discord'—clipped form of *debate*.

22. Cf. *Proverbial Maxims*, v. 11: "Ane man quhen he began suld think on the end." (*Maitland Folio MS.*, ed., Craigie, STS, n.s. 7, p. 159.)

29, 30. This couplet occurs also, as four short lines, at the close of No. 25 above.

60. Praise of Contentment with Little

Unique. *Index* 1218. A familiar theme in the Middle Ages. *Take Tyme in Tyme*, a single stanza (no. cxxii) of the *Maitland Folio MS.*, ends with practically the same lines:

> Bettir is to suffir and fortoun to abyd
> Than haistalie to clym and suddenlie to slyd.

61-66. Ænigmata

These riddles occur on a fly-leaf opposite p. 1 in MS. Dd.5.76 (see No. 4) in an early sixteenth-century hand. The writing, extremely small and fine, suggests the hand of the Reidpath MS. (L1.5.10).

This type of riddle, with its *double entendre*, belongs to an ancient tradition. Similar ambiguous verses are to be found in Kemble (*The Dialogue of Salomon and Saturnus, with an historical introduction*, L: Ælfric Soc., 1848). Older versions of the *sheath* and the *glove* riddles occur among the riddles of the Exeter Book. Frederick Tupper (*Riddles of the Exeter Book*, p. xxv) well sums up the matter:

> By far the most numerous of all riddles of lapsing or varying solutions are those distinctively popular and unrefined problems whose sole excuse for being (or lack of excuse) lies in the double meaning and coarse suggestion. And the reason for this uncertainty of answer is at once apparent. The formally stated solution is so overshadowed by the obscene subject implicitly presented in each limited motive of the riddle, that little attention is paid to the aptness of this. It is after all only a pretense, not the chief concern of the jest. Almost any other answer will serve equally well as a grave and decent anti-climax to the smut and horse laughter of the riddle; so every country, indeed every section supplies different tags to the same repulsive queries. Wossidlo's material garnered directly from the folk furnishes a dozen examples. . . . These instances abundantly prove the absurdity of dogmatizing over the answers to the Anglo-Saxon riddles of this class.

See also Riddles 26, 45, 46, 55, 62, 63, 64, and the notes to them.

Tupper (*MLN*, XVIII, 103) also mentions analogues to the Exeter Book riddles of this type. "To these," he says, "We should expect to find many parallels in the folk-literature, and we are not disappointed." Analogues occur in fifteenth-century French riddles, in Low German, Icelandic, and Lithuanian. Tupper specifically notes that the *Dough* riddle appears in various forms in modern Germany, in a Lithuanian collection, and in fifteenth-century Germany, and that it is known to English peasants. I myself have heard riddles of this *genre* from Swedes, Italians, Germans, and Greeks; indeed, those about the "Eye" and the "Razor" were among the favorite jokes of the schoolboys of my grammar-school days.

Several of the riddles of this present volume bear close resemblances to the *double entendre* riddles of the Exeter Book: No. 65 to Exeter Book 26 ("onion"); No. 66 to EB 45 ("Sheath" or "Key"); no. 68, the answer to which is illegible in the MS., is undoubtedly, it seems to me, a variant or analogue of Tupper's 55 ("Churn").

No. 65. ?test 'a potsherd?'

No. 66. *placht*, cf. *OED*, *s.v.* PLACKET.

67. When I Complain

Not listed by Brown.

The *Index* 3958 description "A Lover's Plaint—a quatrain and a bob" is apparently inexact.

Evidently the work of an amateur versifier. The Booke of Ipotyse ends at fol. 99r and is followed, fol. 99v, by a paragraph in another hand: "Resone will howe so lyfyth take hede thinke on thinge notable to yᵉ yy." Next, in the same hand, comes No. 68, preceded by the heading, somewhat fainter than the text of the poem itself, "And y com." James (*Cat.*, I, 76), with masterful understatement concludes his remarks on the poem with "The end is obscurely written."

The obscurity of some of the lines, as well as the lack of coherence, is due, I believe, to the demands of the rime scheme. The writer seems far more concerned with keeping to this than with making good sense.

68. For to Pente

Unique. *Index* 853. This poem is followed at 144v by *In ffull grett hevenesse myn hert ys pwyght*, printed by Brown, *Rel. Lyr. XVth Cent.*, pp. 266-68. The *Univ. Lib. Cat.* description of this entire MS. is unsatisfactory; it does not mention No. 68 at all. See Hammond, *Manual*, pp. 343 ff., and Robbins' note, *loc. cit.*

"Continuance of Remembrance," printed in *Rel. Ant.*, I, 25-26, from the same codex, foll. 138v-139r, is arranged on the page in exactly the same way as No. 68, except that in the former the writing is neater and the scribal lines indicating rime-fellows are used more generously.

Continvaunce	With owte endyng
Of remembraunce	
Doth me penaunce	ffor your partynge
and grete greuaunce	

etc.

For the verse form see also Chaucer's *Anelida*, vv. 272-280, 333-341.

APPENDIX

Stowe's Deviations from the Trinity MS.
No. 48

1. Ladie, bee
2. seldome, soueraine
3. beautie
4. Remebryng, well
5. brou3t
6. faire, is, angelike
7. beautie
8. For
9. Face, all, enough, fairnesse
10. Her iyen
11. Rauinish yelowe, is, sounitresse
12. comelinesse
13. Soche quantite
14. least, is
15. been ibent
16. betil browed, with all
17. her witte, simple
18. is, childe, all
19. is, thicke, her, small
20. Her fingers been little, nothing
21. skin is, Oxes
22. Thereto, is, wise, daliaunce
23. beset
24. her, it doeth, displesaunce
25. For, saieth is said
26. That when there be mo then she and I
27. still
28. should, goodlie, speache spill
29. slothe none shall
30. diligent, is, vertulesse
31. busie, aie, all, undresse
32. Ape, is
33. Harnet, pitelesse
34. With, is, wise, circumspecte
35. prudence none her folie

36. Is it not ioye, soche one, her
37. Within, bounds, great tendernesse
38. Should, sadde
39. all
41. yeres ten and fiue
42. I trowe there are not many soche aliue
43. Jesu, synfull soule
44. nis, all this worlde liuing
45. Like, her, would
46. pleaseth mine hart y^t
47. Whose soule, his blis
48. first her formed
49. For, well

Explicit the discriuing of a faire Ladie

No. 49

Title: An other Balade

1. Mossie, youre
2. whiche no man dare plucke awaie nor
3. all, folke, for by
4. Youre floures freshe, fallen awaie
5. right sorie maistresse, your
6. all, forgoten
7. ripe, waxe almoste roten
8-14. Omitted here by Stowe, but printed elsewhere. See notes.
15. Your vglie, deinous and
16. Your iyen, not
17. Your chekes enbolned like a melowe Costard
18. Colour, your brestes Satournad
19. Gilt vpon warantise the colour wil not fade
20. Bawsin buttocked belied like a tonne
21. crie S. Barbary at ye losing of your gōne
22. leude maistres
23. sorowfull
24. The floure of ye barkfate ye foulest of al ye naciō
25. You, little, is myne entent
26. the swert hath I swent you ye smoke hath you shet
27. trow, been laid vpō some kill to drie
28. You, worship, presēt
29. Of al womē I loue you best a m. times fie

BIBLIOGRAPHY

BROWN, CARLETON F. *A Register of Middle English Religious and Didactic Verse* (2 vols.). Oxford, 1916, 1920. (Vol. 1 is the Catalogue of Manuscripts and Vol. 2 the Index of First Lines. The abbreviation *Br*, followed by a number, is employed in the present book to denote the numbered items of Vol. 2.)

——————. *English Lyrics of the Thirteenth Century.* Oxford, 1932.

——————. *Religious Lyrics of the Fifteenth Century.* Oxford, 1939.

——————. *Religious Lyrics of the Fourteenth Century.* Oxford, 1924.

BROWN, CARLETON F., and ROBBINS, ROSSELL HOPE. *The Index of Middle English Verse.* The Index Society, N.Y., 1943. (Herein referred to as *Index.*)

BRUSENDORFF, AAGE. *The Chaucer Tradition.* London, 1925.

BYRNE, SISTER MARIE JOSÉ. *Prolegomena to an Edition of the Works of Decimus Magnus Ausonius.* N.Y., 1916.

CHAMBERS, E. K. and SIDGWICK, F. *Early English Lyrics.* London, 1907.

DYBOSKI, ROMAN. *Songs, Carols, and Other Miscellaneous Poems from MS. Balliol 354* (EETSES, 101). London, 1907.

EVELYN-WHITE, H. G. *Ausonius* (Loeb Libr.). N.Y., 1919.

FURNIVALL, F. J. *Political, Religious, and Love Poems* (EETS 15). London, 1866.

GREENE, RICHARD L. *The Early English Carols.* Oxford, 1935.

HALLIWELL-PHILLIPPS, J. O., and WRIGHT, THOMAS. *Reliquiae Antiquae* (2 vols.). London, 1841-43.

HAMMOND, ELEANOR P. *Chaucer: A Bibliographical Manual.* N.Y., 1908.

——————. *English Verse between Chaucer and Surrey.* Durham, North Carolina, 1927.

C. HARDWICK and H. R. LUARD, editors. *Catalogue of Manuscripts Preserved in the Library of the University of Cambridge.* (6 vols.) Cambridge, 1856-67.

HORSTMANN, CARL. *The Minor Poems of the Vernon MS.* (EETS 98, 117). London, 1892, 1901.

JAMES, MONTAGUE R. *A Descriptive Catalogue of the Manuscripts in the Library of Corpus Christi College, Cambridge.* (2 vols.) Cambridge, 1912.

——————. *A Descriptive Catalogue of the Manuscripts in the Library of Gonville and Caius College, Cambridge.* (2 vols. & supp.) Cambridge, 1907.

——————. *A Descriptive Catalogue of the Manuscripts in the Library of Pembroke College, Cambridge.* Cambridge, 1905.

——————. *A Descriptive Catalogue of the Manuscripts in the Library of St. John's College, Cambridge.* Cambridge, 1913.

——————. *Western Manuscripts in the Library of Emmanuel College, Cambridge. A Descriptive Catalogue.* Cambridge, 1904.

——————. *The Western Manuscripts in the Library of Trinity College, Cambridge. A Descriptive Catalogue* (4 vols.). Cambridge, 1900.

KANE, GEORGE. *Middle English Literature.* London, 1949.

MACAULAY, G. C. *The English Works of John Gower* (EETSES 82). London, 1901.

MACCRACKEN, HENRY N. *The Minor Poems of John Lydgate* (EETSES 107, 192). London, 1911, 1934.

MOORE, ARTHUR K. *The Secular Lyric in Middle English.* Lexington, Kentucky, 1951.

PATTERSON, FRANK A. *The Middle English Penitential Lyric.* N.Y., 1911.

PEIPER, RUDOLF. *Decimi Magni Avsonii Opvscvla.* Leipzig, 1876.

ROBBINS, R. H. "Levation Prayers in Middle English Verse," *Modern Philology,* 40: 131-46.

————. "Popular Prayers in Middle English Verse", *Modern Philology,* 36: 337-50.

————. "Private Prayers in Middle English Verse," *Studies in Philology,* 36: 467-75.

————. *Secular Lyrics of the XIV and XV Centuries.* Oxford, 1952.

SKEAT, W. W. *The Complete Works of Geoffrey Chaucer* (6 vols.). Oxford, 1899.

————. *Chaucerian and Other Pieces.* Oxford, 1897. (Herein referred to as *Ox.Ch.,VII.*)

STEELE, ROBERT. *Secrees of Old Philisoffres* (EETSES 66). L, 1894.

————. *Three Prose Versions of the Secreta Secretorum* (EETSES 74). L, 1898.

TUPPER, FREDERICK. *The Riddles of the Exeter Book* (Albion Series). N.Y., 1910.

WELLS, J. E. *A Manual of the Writings in Middle English 1050-1400.* New Haven, 1916. (Eight supplements.)

WHITING, E. K. *The Poems of John Audelay* (EETS 184). L, 1930.

WRIGHT, THOMAS. *Songs and Carols* (Percy Soc.). L, 1847.

INDEX OF FIRST LINES

	Number	Page
A vidue pouere was & freo	54	49
Abel wes looset in treunesse	24	25
Al fram vuele þinge me schulde iesus þat may	34	28
Alas, alas, and alas why	40	31
Alas what planet was y born vndir	41	32
Almyghty god fader of heuen	1C	3
Allmyʒtty god fadyr of heuen	1A	1
Almyʒty god fadyr of heuen	1B	2
Also crist steʒ vp hastely	38	29
And as þou wolde c . . . en þis wyse	4	6
And ye will please god gretly	25	25
As in yow resstyth my Ioy and comfort	42	32
Backe bent smocke rent	65	54
Be meke & meylde yn hert & towng	20	21
Bi þis tokninge of þare rode	35	28
Consideryng effectually the gret diuersite	53	44
Cryste crosse me spede & seynt nycolas	3	5
Cur mundus militat sub vana gloria	14	16
Enforce thy wyttes for to lere	55	49
Fyrst whan a man or a woman drynkes more	21	22
ffor I wend when any foly me felte	39	30
ffor to pente and after repente	68	56
Heyl boe þov marie ful of godes grace	30	27
Heyle fairest þat euyr god fonde	10	11
Heyle god ye schilde	12	14
Heil marie ful of wynne	11	14
Haue mynde on the blys þat neuer schall blyne	23	24
Hiegh towres by strong wyndes full lowe be cast	60	53
How darest thow swere or be so bold also	26	26
I haue a hole aboue my knee	63	54
I haue a lady where so she be	48	38
I haue a thing and roughe yt is	64	54
I may well sygh for greuous ys my payne	43	33
Jhesu mercy and graunt mercy	5	8
In toe þine hondes louerd bitech yh gost minñe	33	28
Knyʒtes in travayle for to serve	47	38

	Number	Page
Lady of pite for þ, sorowes þat þou haddest	13	14
Liuis firist & licames hele	27	26
Man yff thow wylt my mercy gete	2	3
Myn oȝen deþ and cristes and mi wikedhede	36	28
Natura pingues isti sunt atque forantes	58	99
O dethe whylum dysplesant to nature	45	34
O man vnkynde	9	11
O mosy quince hangyng by youre stalke	49	40
O þou fortune why art þou so inconstaunt	46	35
Of yiftis large in love hathe gret delite	58	50
Vre fader in heuene yhalȝed bo þy name	29	27
Penaunce is in herte reusinge	28	26
Prute ȝisscinge sleuþe wreþe and onde	31	27
Salamon seýth ther is none accorde	59	52
Schrude and fede and drenche and herborwe þe pouere	37	29
The vnware woo that commeth on gladnesse	57	50
þe saule haskis ryȝt as writin is in storie	15	18
Ther ys a thyng as I suppose	66	54
Ther was a ladie leaned her back to a wall	61	53
Thow gracious lord graunt me memory	6	8
þou þat sellest þe worde of god	51	41
Thurwe my ryȝt hande a nayle was driuen	7	9
Trusty seldom to their ffrendys uniust	52	43
Two stones hathe yt or els yt is wrong	62	53
We fynde wryttyn X thynges sere	22	23
What helpith it man to be vnstable	56	49
When fishes in the water leve their swymmyng	50	41
Whan I compley[n]e ther is no Resone	67	55
Wenne þin eyen beit ihut	19	21
Whan thy hed quakes, *memento*	16	19
Whan thyn heed shaketh *memento*	18	20
When þi hed whaketh / *memento*	17	20
Where y haue chosyn stedefast woll y be	44	34
With a garlande of thornes kene	8	10
Wolcome louerd in likninge of bred	32	28